Lost Restaurants

OF

LINCOLN

NEBRASKA

Lost Restaurants of Lincoln Nebraska

JEFF KORBELIK

AMERICAN PALATE

Published by American Palate
A Division of The History Press
Charleston, SC
www.historypress.com

First published 2018

Manufactured in the United States

ISBN 9781467139496

Library of Congress Control Number: 9781467139496

For Rebecca, my dining companion

Contents

Contents

Acknowledgements

Though I wanted to, I wasn't sure I had the time or the inclination to write a book. But Lincoln historian Jim McKee, who has written and published a book or two over the years, convinced me that I could do it. So my first thank-you goes to Jim, who said that "everyone has at least one book in them." In addition to encouragement, Jim provided historical background and photographs.

A big thank-you goes to my former employer the *Lincoln Journal Star* and editor Dave Bundy, who allowed me access to the newspaper's library, where much of the material was found for the book. Before the *Journal Star* went digital in 1996, librarians clipped stories and filed them in envelopes, making it easier for reporters to do research back in the day. I spent a lot of time with those envelopes. Along those lines, newspapers.com also proved to be a valuable resource in confirming many dates.

My friend Jill Morstad, an English professor, edited many of my chapters to make sure I didn't screw up my grammar or use too many commas. I'm indebted to the folks at The History Press—Candice Lawrence, Artie Crisp and Abigail Fleming, who helped shepherd the book through all its phases.

I also wanted to thank the Lincoln restaurateurs who shared their their first-person stories. They include Pearl Kuhl and her family, John and Despina Kazas, Nader Sepahpur, Bob Campbell, Bob Jergensen, Norma Latzel and her family, Maggie Pleskac, Diane Kann and Mark Lohmeier, Kay Brestel and her family, Matt Smith, Kristina Tiebel, Mike Alesio and

Tony Messineo and Daniel and Rene Longoria. I had a blast revisiting Lincoln's culinary past through them.

And finally my wife, Rebecca, gets the biggest shout-out. She wanted me to do this more than I did, and I'm thankful for her encouragement. Plus, she scanned nearly all my photos, saving me a bunch of time and stress. Now we can go to the movies.

Introduction

It's funny how we perceive the world as children.

When I was kid, I thought it was odd that all restaurants didn't have tabletop telephones the way King's Food Hosts did. I also remember thinking Tastee Inn & Out's drive-thru window on the passenger side of a car was normal. My father was busy driving, so having my mom handle the transaction—she was in charge of the money anyway—seemed practical.

As I discovered later, King's phones and Tastee's backward drive-thru is what made these two restaurants extraordinary in Lincoln—that and their tasty food. King's became known for its burgers and cheese frenchees, and Tastee's, of course, had the loose-meat sandwiches and onion chips and dip.

So when The History Press recruited me to write a book about Lincoln's lost restaurants, I thought about what criteria to use for inclusion. Obviously, the restaurants had to be no longer operating, so such classics as Lee's Chicken Restaurant—currently the city's oldest restaurant—Runza, Billy's and Tico's wouldn't be on the list.

I finally decided to include restaurants that had interesting stories to share, stories that readers may or may not know about them. Many know that former Nebraska football coach and athletic director Bob Devaney spent a lot of time at the Legionnaire Club, but how many know that Ken Eddy's owner Eddy Gold fought a battle with the Lincoln Garden Club to have a stone settee removed from his property at 48th and O Streets?

I also wanted to make it a mix of classic and contemporary restaurants, with some of the newer ones being among those I reviewed in my twenty-plus years as the *Lincoln Journal Star* food critic.

The oldest is the Acme Chili Parlor, which A.C. Christopulos, believed to be Lincoln's first Greek immigrant, opened in Lincoln in 1909—a time when many of the city's eating establishments were boardinghouses. The youngest is Maggie's Vegetarian Cafe, which closed in December 2017 after more than seventeen years. The café arguably was the city's most successful vegetarian and vegan restaurant.

I broke my list down into two categories—restaurants and supper clubs and cafés, diners and drive-ins—and chose 32 to write about. Of course, given Lincoln's rich dining history, the number could have been 132.

Maybe those can be included in any future volumes about Lincoln's lost restaurants.

RESTAURANTS AND SUPPER CLUBS

Alice's Restaurant

The line outside of Alice's Restaurant was a typical sight in College View at noon on Sundays.

When it first opened in 1958 as Alice's Cafe, the restaurant at 4013 South 48th Street seated 25. By May 1974, seating had grown to 160 after three expansions.

And still there were lines.

Nobody was happier to see that than Alice Schroeder herself.

"People said to me 'raise the prices, and you'll cut the waiting lines,' but I can't soak people….I could, but I'd rather have the waiting lines," the restaurant owner told the *Sunday Journal Star*. "For volume, you keep food quality up, you keep service, but you keep prices moderate."

That proved to be Schroeder's key to success, as she, her husband, Carl, and their children—Erling, Cordell and Bernice—built a small restaurant empire in Lincoln. At one point during the 1970s—from 1974 to 1976—the Schroeders operated three restaurants in Lincoln: the original in College View, one at 3822 Normal Boulevard and the crown jewel at 211 North 70th.

The latter restaurant, which opened in May 1974, was a $300,000 structure with seating for more than two hundred and contained a separate bake shop, Alice's Oven, where those delicious homemade pies were made.

Schroeder rarely gave interviews, but she opened up to the *Sunday Journal Star* for a story touting the opening of the North 70th Street restaurant. She told reporter Gene Kelly the reason for her success was "food I personally stand behind…yes, the food.

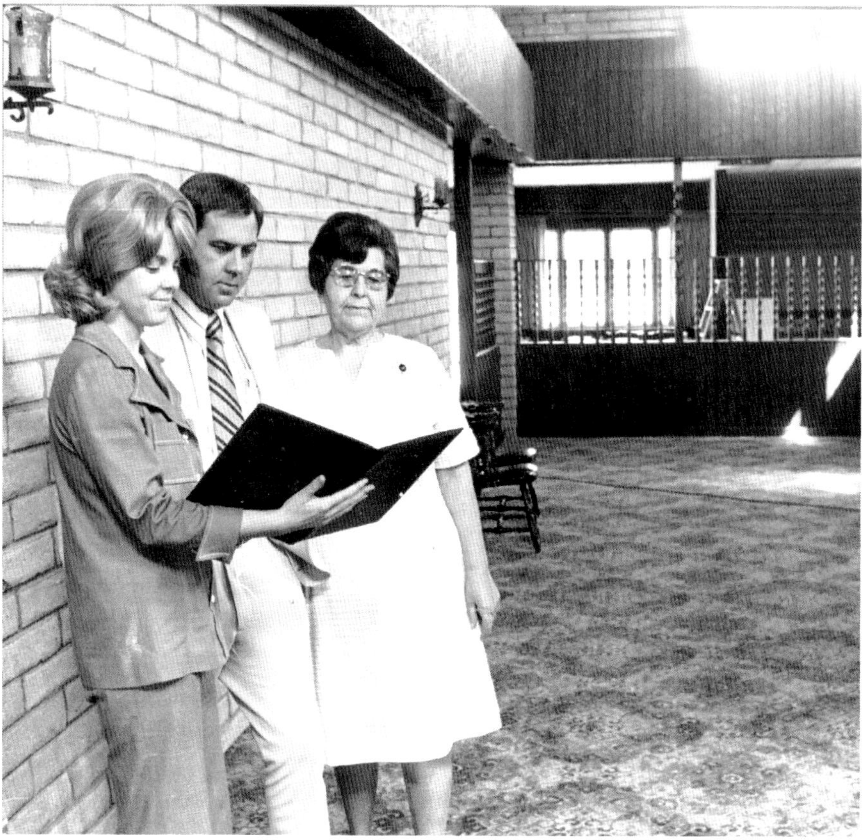

Alice Schroeder (*right*) scans the menu for her restaurant in May 1974. *Courtesy of the* Lincoln Journal Star.

"Personality," she went on to say. "You yourself—the owner, waitresses who give of themselves. Who smile. These attitudes are part of business. A waitress serving you one of the most enjoyable things in the world....[I]f she isn't pleasant—no smoke, poor service—it can spoil the food."

Schroeder told the newspaper she learned to cook for large groups as the eldest girl in a farm family of six kids. At threshing time, as many as fifteen hungry workers became part of the family for banquet-style meals. Her first experience with commercial food was running a small restaurant in tiny Gackle, North Dakota, where she and Carl farmed.

Alice and Carl moved to Lincoln in the 1950s. Carl worked as a floor-coverings installer before he and Alice opened Alice's Cafe in 1958. They remained active in ownership until turning over the reins to their son Erling in the early 1970s. By 1974, when the North 70th Street restaurant opened, Alice was serving as a consultant.

The restaurants became known for home-style fare, southern fried chicken, roast beef, meatloaf, chicken-fried steak and hot apple pie.

"You back your food," Alice said. "You try it before you serve it. You show the cook how to make it to your standards…and I mean home cooking."

The second store, at 3822 Normal Boulevard, operated from August 1969 to February 1971 and from September 1974 to around August 1976. In between, it was a restaurant called Shondele. The original Alice's closed in 1981.

"Through the years the Alice's on South 48th had its own evolvement as a business," Erling told the *Lincoln Journal*. "But as time went on, we found that the Alice's on North 70th and the sister corporation Crockett's has become the mainstay of our business."

Crockett's operated from 1979 to 1985 at 3201 Pioneers Boulevard. Erling sold the North 70th Street restaurant in July 1987 to investor Richard Saduikis, who operated it as Alice's for a short time before changing the name to Cambridge Coffee, Tea & Spice House. Carl passed away on November 13, 1982, at age seventy-five. Alice died on February 8, 2000, at age eighty-eight.

As of this writing, the original Alice's Restaurant is home to a tattoo parlor and a karate studio, while Mazatlan Mexican Restaurant resides at the North 70th Street location.

Alice's Apple Fritters

4 cups flour
½ cup sugar
2 tablespoons baking powder
½ teaspoon salt
2 eggs, beaten
1 ⅔ cups milk
⅓ cup orange juice
¼ teaspoon vanilla
2 cups diced apples

Combine flour, sugar, baking powder and salt in a bowl and set aside. In a larger bowl, beat eggs until foamy. Add milk, orange juice, vanilla and apples. Fold flour mixture into liquid, stirring gently to moisten. Do not beat or over mix. If batter is over-stirred, the fritters will not be fluffy. Using a tablespoon, drop mixture into oil that has been preheated to 300 degrees in a deep fryer. Fry for 5 minutes or until golden brown. Drain on paper towel and roll in powdered sugar. Makes about 2½ dozen.

—Chef's Corner, the *Lincoln Star*, September 14, 1983

Crane River

When Crane River opened in 1992, it quickly became known for its craft beer, diverse menu and signature art piece—a 26½-foot-long quilt depicting a Platte River Valley scene featuring two sandhill cranes.

Owners Kristina Tiebel and Linda Vescio commissioned Nebraska quiltmaker Shelly Burge to create the piece, which hung in the bar area on the north wall until the restaurant closed in May 2003.

"It was Linda's idea," Tiebel said.

> *We knew we wanted the place to be wide open with lots of glass, and the brewery was glass.* [The restaurant] *had a lot of hard surfaces.*
>
> *We wanted something that would soften it up a little big to absorb some of that sound that traveled. We wanted to have something to do with Nebraska. Most of our beers were named after a Nebraska thing.*
>
> *We wanted cranes and the Platte River.*

Crane River opened in October 1992 as Lincoln's second brewpub, and Burge's quilt went up two months later. (Lazlo's was the city's—and state's—first brewpub, opening in 1991).

According to a *Lincoln Journal* article, Burge took 319 hours to design and piece the quilt together in her rural Lincoln home. She used hundreds of fabric pieces and two thousand yards of clear nylon thread for the top quilting. At more than six feet wide, it became the largest quilt she had done up to that point.

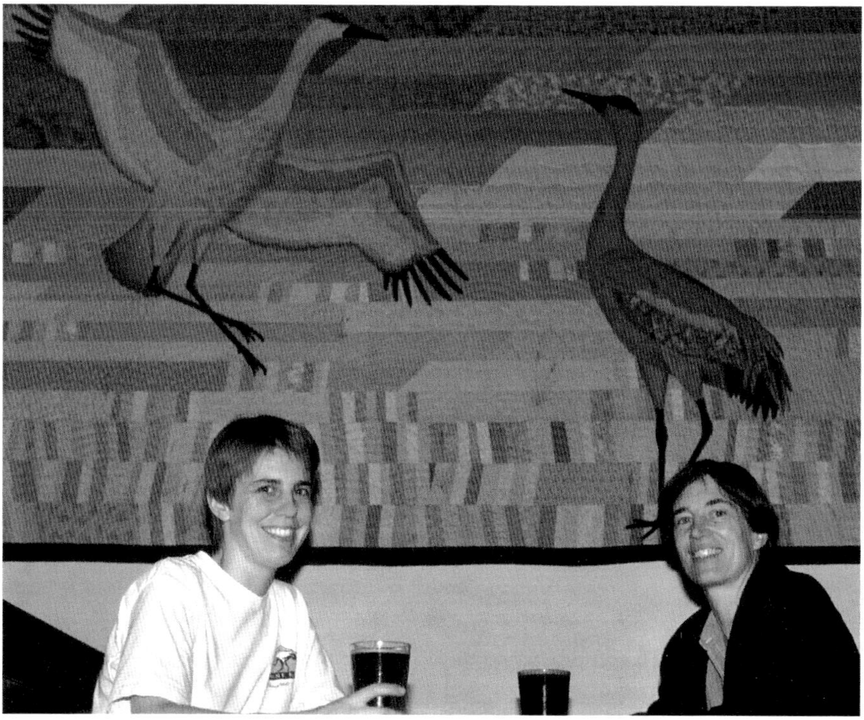

Crane River owners Kristina Tiebel (*left*) and Linda Vescio enjoy homemade beers in front of the colorful quilt commissioned for the restaurant. *Courtesy of Kristina Tiebel.*

"I do a lot of miniature quilts, less than 2-foot square, so it was big change from those," she told the *Journal* in December 1992. "But a lot of my quilts are based on Nebraska themes, so I was used to working with Nebraska nature."

Tiebel and Vescio turned to Burge after seeing some of her earlier prizewinning creations.

"I was really honored that they think of quilting as a piece of artwork," Burge told the *Journal*. "The colors are very muted in there, and when that went up it just seemed to add color all through the room."

The quilt, Tiebel said, became a draw.

"We had a lot of quilt tourists," she said. "We once had like a busload of fifty people to come to see the quilt. They drank tea. They were not at all interested in Crane River, just the quilt."

But there were just as many people interested in Crane River's beers and food.

Tiebel and Vescio became acquainted through the University of Nebraska–Lincoln's biology department. Tiebel was a lab technician, and Vescio helped run a field station. They began homebrewing together because "there really wasn't any good beer in Lincoln at the time." In the late 1980s, they attended a microbrewers convention in Denver, with thoughts of starting their own operation.

"We went to see if it went great, and it did," Tiebel said. Back then, to sell your own beer, you had two options—to sell it in a restaurant or as a distributor. She continued,

> [Distributorship] *didn't appeal to us because that just sounded like being salesmen. Linda had worked in restaurants before, but I never had. Maybe if I had, I wouldn't have done it. In the beginning, I intended to just be the brewer and Linda was basically going to run the restaurant.*
>
> *When we got open, it was just clearly dumb for one of the two people who cared the most to be locked away in the brewery all the time by herself, so I moved out of that role and became the "executive brewer" then. I said "Hello" to the brewer and made sure he knew what to do.*

The duo had a reported twenty-eight investors, including Wynkoop Brewing Company in Denver, which shared its expertise in beer making and food service. Some of the early beer, the English bitter (ESB), for example, and food recipes came from the Denver pub.

Crane River operated on the northeast corner of 11th and P Streets. Tiebel and Vescio spent a reported $300,000 remodeling the nine-thousand-square-foot space on the ground floor of the historic Lincoln Commercial Club Building, which was designed in 1911 and finished in 1912. They restored the original storefront windows, corner doorways and mosaic tile floor.

In addition to the quilt, notable features included a concrete bar inlaid with rock from the Platte River Valley, curved hardwood benches and a gray dining area carpet made of fibers spun from recycled plastic pop bottles.

The menu, as *Journal* dining critic Tom Ineck noted, was going "to test most Nebraska diners' sense of adventure." It boasted a mix of vegetarian dishes, burgers, British pub food (bangers and mash, fish and chips) and exotic meats.

"We were warned a lot, initially, that you can't sell lamb in Lincoln and you can't sell anything odd, that we'd never sell any buffalo and we'd never sell any elk, and that we were being foolish," Vescio told the *Journal* after

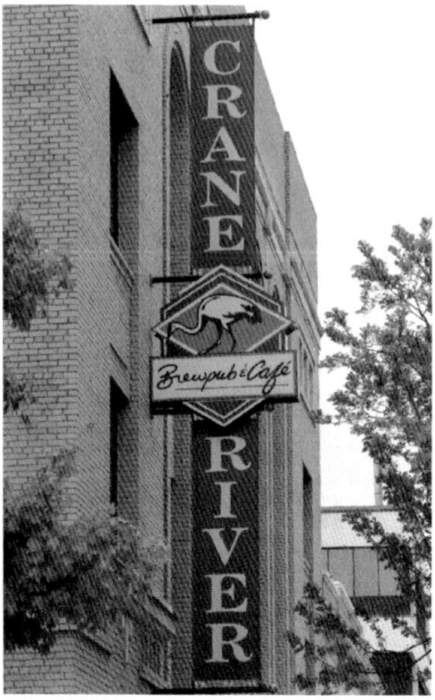

Crane River opened in 1992 at the corner of 11th and P Streets. *Courtesy of the* Lincoln Journal Star.

opening. "I think people in Lincoln are a lot more adventuresome than they're given credit for."

The beer menu featured a mix of English- and German-style ales and beers, with a Nebraska reference tied to many of them. The taps poured such beers as a Whooping Wheat, Zlate Pivo (a golden Czech beer recognizing Nebraska's large Czech heritage), Homestead Pale Ale, the Sod House and a Good Life Stout.

When it opened, Crane River garnered some national attention.

"It was kind of new for women to open a brewery," Tiebel said about the then male-dominated industry. "I don't know if it mattered to Lincoln that much, but we got a lot of press for that—not necessarily in Lincoln, but all the brewery magazines had a feature. We had a lot of beer tourists because of that."

In May 2003, Tiebel and Vescio closed Crane River, citing burnout.

"We thought over time we would be able to hire some help to do the work, but we were never able to do that," Tiebel said. "It got to be where we had been working too hard for too long."

Misty's, a longtime Lincoln restaurant with roots dating back to 1964, opened in Crane River's spot. The steakhouse ceased making beer in 2017, opening its taps instead to a variety of local and national craft brewers.

Burge's quilt now hangs in Hardin Hall on the University of Nebraska–Lincoln's East Campus.

"It was one of the really big experiences of my life," Tiebel said.

> *I learned a tremendous amount of stuff and really enjoyed meeting all the people I got to meet through the restaurant, the employees, our customers and all that stuff. It was great. It was something so hugely different from what I had done before. Just about every experience with was something brand new. That's a really good thing to do in your life…once. I look back fondly, but I don't miss it.*

Nor does she miss making beer.

"Brewing is fun hobby, but now you find good beer everywhere," she said. "You can have a lot more variety with a lot less work. Back when we were homebrewing, you couldn't buy good beer hardly."

Drumstick

Before R.E.M. charted such hits as "Losing My Religion," "Stand" and "The One I Love," the alternative rock band toured the country, playing in small clubs to hundreds instead of thousands. In 1982, two years after coming together in an abandoned church in Athens, Georgia, the band performed in Lincoln for the first time at a fried chicken restaurant called the Drumstick. This was a year before R.E.M. released *Murmur*, the record *Rolling Stone* would name the best of 1983.

In an interview with the *Lincoln Journal*, R.E.M. guitarist Peter Buck fondly remembered his introduction to the Lincoln eatery, which doubled as one of the city's premier live music venues:

> *The Drumstick I figured would be a little punk club in town.... We pulled up and looked inside and there were people eating chicken and it was "Wow, this is great." There was an 80-year-old lady there with three or four kids, maybe they were her grandkids. They were sitting there as we were setting up for the sound check.*
>
> *We play loud, we always have. We started tuning up and making noise and the lady tore up a napkin and put pieces in all the kids' ears and kept on eating right through our sound check. We couldn't believe this lady kept on calmly eating chicken through all this. I went down and said "Hello" and shook her hand afterward.*

This story isn't unusual, largely because this wasn't just any fried chicken.

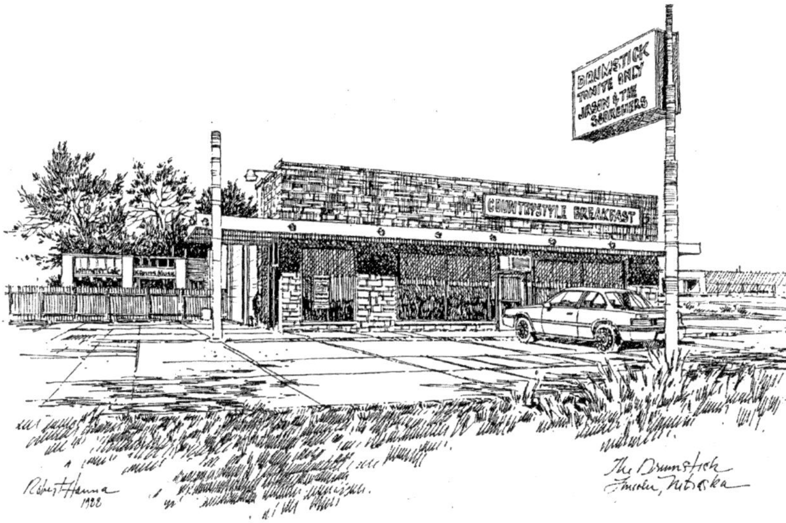

Robert Hanna sketched the Drumstick, with the sign advertising Jason & The Scorchers performing "tonite only." *Courtesy of Diane Kann.*

Starting in 1966, when Henry "Jerry" Lohmeier took over the restaurant at 547 North 48th Street, the Drumstick became many Lincoln diners' destination for chicken battered in flour and buttermilk and deep fried to a juicy crispness.

So a little loud music wasn't going to hinder anybody's enjoyment.

"I remember this one little old couple," said Lohmeier's daughter Diane Kann. Diane worked at the restaurant and co-owned it with her brother Tim after their father retired in 1979.

> *We used to have a lot of regulars on Sunday morning or Monday and Tuesday nights. And this little old couple would order two No. 5s, a leg and a thigh, and I remember taking them their food and when I came back they had eaten every speck of what was on that bone. They had eaten the meat, the gristle, the cartilage, everything. All that was left was these bare bones.*

An army cook, Lohmeier opened a bar and grill in his Sutton, Nebraska hometown following World War II. He moved his family to Lincoln in 1954

GOLDEN FRIED CHICKEN

Served with Cole Slaw, and Texas Toast. Choice of Hash Browns, French Fries, or Baked Potato

NO. 1	REGULAR ORDER—Three Pieces of Chicken	2.85
NO. 2	ONE-HALF CHICKEN—All White Meat	3.50
NO. 3	ONE-HALF CHICKEN— Dark and White Meat	3.40
NO. 4	ONE-QUARTER CHICKEN—All White Meat	2.60
NO. 5	ONE-QUARTER CHICKEN—Leg and Thigh	2.55
NO. 6	ALL LIVERS—Six Livers Fried Golden and Delicious	2.60
NO. 7	ALL GIZZARDS—Six Gizzards Fried Golden and Delicious	2.60
NO. 8	MIXED GIBLETS—Three Livers and Three Gizzards	2.60
NO. 9	ALL THIGHS—Three Meaty Chicken Thighs	2.90
NO. 10	ALL LEGS—Four Pieces of Everyone's Favorite, the Drumstick	2.90
NO. 11	CHILD'S PORTION—Two Drumsticks for the Little One	1.95
NO. 12	BUCKET OF CHICKEN—Ten Pieces of Chicken, can be served family style	7.25

A LA CARTE CHICKEN ORDERS

ONE BREAST—1.85 LEG—.85 THIGH—.95 GIBLETS—.30 each

SANDWICHES, SALADS, AND SOUPS

All sandwiches served with cole slaw

STEAK SANDWICH— Served on Toast with Lettuce and Mayo	2.50
BACON & TOMATO—On Toast with Crisp Lettuce	2.00
FISH SANDWICH—On Toasted Bun with Tartar Sauce	1.25
HAMBURGER—¼ pound	1.00
CHEESBURGER—¼ pound	1.25
HAM SANDWICH	1.50
HAM & AMERICAN CHEESE	1.65
GRILLED HAM & CHEESE	1.75
GRILLED CHEESE	1.00
TOSSED DINNER SALAD	.85
COTTAGE CHEESE SALAD	.65
SOUP OF THE DAY	
Bowl	.95
Cup	.70
CLAM CHOWDER (Fridays Only)	
Bowl	1.25
Cup	1.00

DINNERS

(Served with Choice of Potato, Tossed Salad, Texas Toast & Honey)

CLUB STEAK—8 oz. Sirloin	5.95
PETITE CLUB STEAK—5 oz. Sirloin	4.25
LIVER AND ONIONS—Beef Liver Grilled with Onions	2.75
CHOPPED SIRLOIN—8 oz. Ground Sirloin Steak	3.25
CHICKEN FRIED STEAK—8 oz. Breaded Tenderized Steak	3.50
FILLET OF FISH PLATE— Golden Fillet of Fish	2.75
FRIED SHRIMP— Six Shrimp with Cocktail Sauce	4.00
SEAFOOD PLATTER—Fish Fillet, Three Shrimp, Three Oysters with Tartar & Cocktail Sauce	4.95
FRIED OYSTERS—Six oysters with Tartar Sauce	3.75
PORK CHOPS—Two Center Cut Pork Chops	4.25

DESSERTS

STRAWBERRY SHORTCAKE with WHIPPED CREAM	.85
CARROT CAKE with Cream Cheese Icing	.65
ICE CREAM	.50

BEVERAGES

MILK	.40 &.70
BUTTERMILK	.40
HOT CHOCOLATE	.45
COFFEE	.35
TEA	.35
SANKA	.35
COKE, SPRITE	
Glass	.45
Pitcher	2.25
PITCHER OF BEER (Old Style)	2.50
DRAWS (Old Style)	.75

Enjoy a glass of beer or your favorite cocktail with your meal.

ANY ORDER INDIVIDUALLY BOXED TO TAKE OUT

The Drumstick's menu featured twelve items based around its famous fried chicken. *Courtesy of Diane Kann.*

and worked as a short-order cook at Foster's Cafe at 27th and Cornhusker before buying the nearby Kent Cafe.

"They would have this great fried chicken dinner, roast beef dinners, baked ham dinners, Swiss steak dinners," Diane said. "This really fabulous food. They made these fabulous cinnamon rolls, pecan rolls and cream pies....We would get all the leftovers, the day old stuff."

Diane and brother Mark Lohmeier said construction on Cornhusker Highway "destroyed the business," forcing Lohmeier to close the Kent Cafe. He then took over Calumet Cafe at 10th and Q Streets and ran it as a breakfast and lunch place, delivering cinnamon rolls around town.

"Then the road closed down there and it went under," Diane said.

In 1966, Lohmeier struck a deal with Bob Hayes to buy the Drumstick, which had then been open a couple of years. Diane and Mark said their mother, Victoria, who was friends with Bob's wife, helped facilitate the deal.

"My dad's reputation was somewhat tarnished because these businesses had failed," said Mark, who also worked at the Drumstick. "Bob Hayes wasn't real interested in letting my dad take his place over. My mom brokered the deal and said he's more than capable in taking the place over."

Lohmeier did take over the restaurant and inherited the chicken recipe. At the beginning, Lohmeier operated the Drumstick from 6:00 a.m. to 8:00 p.m. daily, but he soon added an overnight service, realizing there was money to be made from hungry after-hours diner. Nobody else really, Mark and Diane said, offered twenty-four-hour service inside the city limits.

"That was when it really became popular because the bar crowd started rolling in," Diane said. "He had a nice business for breakfast, lunch and dinner, but then the nighttime business...there was nobody doing that. They just rocked on the weekends. There would be lines of people out there. It was really something."

In the early 1970s, Lohmeier bought out the laundromat next door and expanded. He also increased the parking lot when a used-car dealership moved its operation. The Drumstick got its first taste of music in August 1978 when local band Little Jimmy Valentine and the Heart Murmurs played a wedding reception for Lohmeier's daughter Cathy, who also worked at the restaurant and had a hand in running it.

Then tragedy struck.

In October 1978, Lohmeier's wife, Victoria, died in an automobile accident. Lohmeier asked his son Tim, who was living in Bar Harbor, Maine, if he would consider returning to Lincoln to help run the restaurant. He agreed. He came back with an idea for the family restaurant.

"He was a fun-seeker," Diane said about her brother, who died in 1998. "He liked to party and knew a lot of musicians. That's when the music thing started."

Eddie & the Clones played the first show in February 1979. Local favorite Charlie Burton & Rock Therapy was the second. But Kann told the *Lincoln Journal* in 1980 that the response "wasn't fantastic, but it was OK." In January 1980, the Drumstick stopped booking bands but resumed in April when the restaurant obtained its liquor license.

Over the next seven years, the Drumstick became one of the Midwest's premier music venues. The restaurant drew such names as R.E.M., Joan Jett and the Blackhearts, the Fabulous Thunderbirds, Georgia Satellites, Soul Asylum, Hüsker Dü, Red Hot Chili Peppers, Black Flag, X, the Meat Puppets, Dwight Yoakam and Steve Earle.

"It was funny," Mark said. "They thought [as R.E.M.'s Peter Buck did] they were playing a nightclub because they were musicians and they pictured in their minds a 'drumstick.' And when they got there, they realized it wasn't a drumstick, but a piece of chicken. It was quite a time."

After playing the night before, many of the bands often returned the next day for breakfast or lunch, depending on when they rolled out of bed.

"They don't look like the other customers," Diane told the *Lincoln Star* in 1984. "A lot of times they'll have leather pants or leather jackets on and long, wild-looking hair."

Lohmeier retired in 1979, turning the restaurant the restaurant over to Diane and Tim. At first, they continued late-night service, reopening the kitchen after the bands finished playing.

"But it didn't work," Mark said. "It would have taken a real coordinated effort to continue both operations, and it wasn't going to happen."

Diane added, "There were so many people at the end of the night, and the place was trashed and it was so hard to flip it back to a restaurant after the music was over. People who were drinking didn't want to leave, and more people were rolling in to eat. It was kind of pandemonium. We did do it for a while."

On August 1, 1987, after twenty-one years of fried chicken and eight years of live music, the Drumstick closed its doors. McDonald's built a restaurant at the site after the building was razed. Diane said the change in the drinking age—raised from twenty to twenty-one in 1985—and higher costs to book bands forced their hand.

"It's just not paying off anymore," Diane told the *Journal Star* in 1987. "Everything went up but the profit."

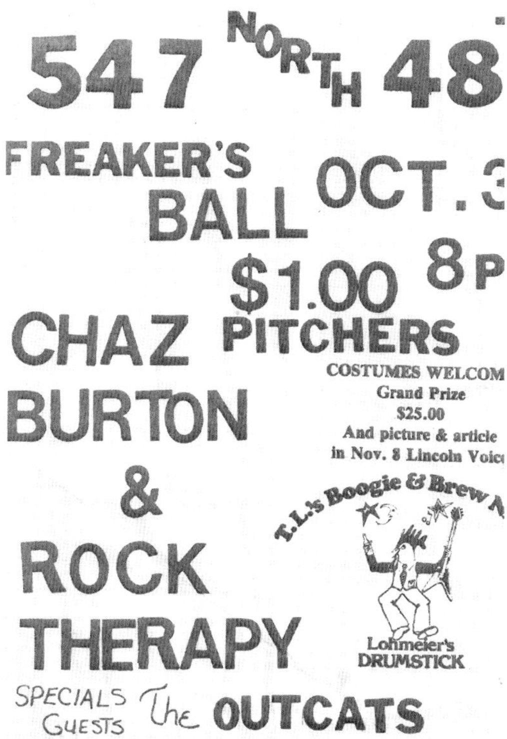

Left: A Drumstick poster advertises one-dollar pitchers of beer and Chaz Burton & Rock Therapy as the entertainment. *Courtesy of Diane Kann.*

Below: The Drumstick as seen in July 1982 at 547 North 48th Street, with the sign advertising the night's band. *Courtesy of the* Lincoln Journal Star.

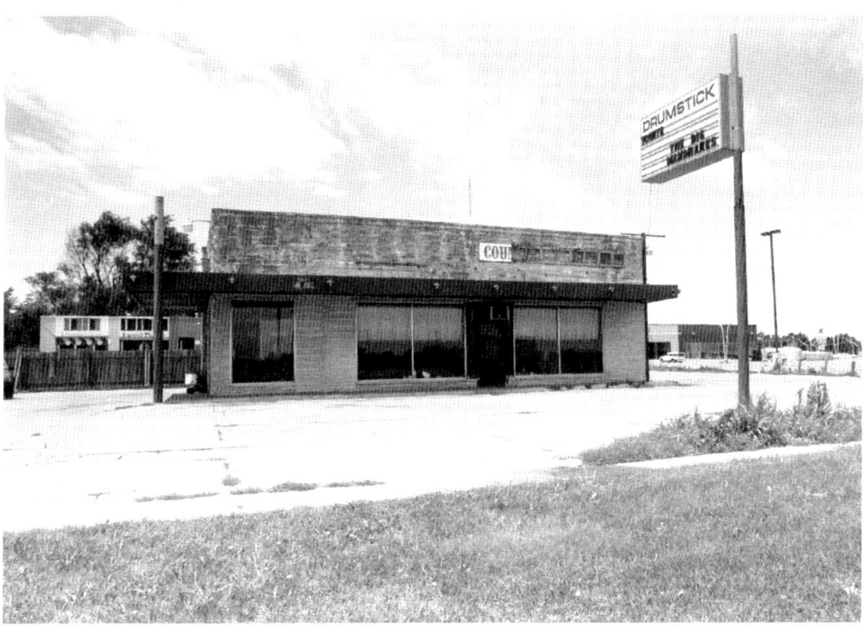

Today, the Drumstick is still fondly remembered. Country star Yoakam mentioned the restaurant/nightclub during his concert in Lincoln in April 2016. There are more than 1,300 people who belong to a "Friends of the Drumstick" Facebook page, and there's even been a couple of reunions over the years.

Drumstick's Fried Chicken

Flour
Salt, to taste
Pepper, to taste
Buttermilk
Water
Chicken pieces

In a bowl, mix flour with salt and pepper. Fill another bowl with equal parts buttermilk and water. Dip and cover chicken in flour mixture and shake. Dip into buttermilk/water. Dip again into flour mixture and shake. Pop into deep-fat fryer and cook until chicken floats.

—Courtesy of Diane Kann and Mark Lohmeier

The Esquire Club

On January 26, 2005, a reader wrote to the *Lincoln Journal Star*'s recipe exchange with a simple request: "Does anyone have the recipe for the dip that the Esquire Club served with their relish tray? Thanks."

A week later, the *Journal Star* printed the response. All six of them.

The six recipes had three ingredients in common: cream cheese, beer and and red food coloring to provide the trademark pink color.

But after that, they varied. Five of the six used horseradish, and the one that didn't was the only one calling for Worcestershire sauce. Three of the recipes used garlic salt; two others used garlic powder instead, and one—the same one with the Worcestershire—called for actual garlic.

Four of the recipes bore the name Esquire Club Dip, one was called simply Esquire Dip and one—NOT the one with the Worcestershire—went all out with a descriptive title: Esquire Club Pink Chip Dip.

At our house, we simply called it "beer dip." The recipe my mother, Virginia Korbelik, has is the one I use to this day.

Beer Dip

1 8-ounce package cream cheese
1 tablespoon horseradish
¼ can of beer
Garlic salt, to taste
Red food coloring, optional

Soften cream cheese in microwave for 15 to 20 seconds. Add horseradish, beer, garlic salt and food coloring and stir until ingredients are blended well and dip is smooth. Serve with potato chips (I prefer wavy) or vegetables.

The beer dip is arguably the most remembered (and requested) recipe from the old Lincoln supper club. The local cookbook *From Soup to Nuts* by Pamela Fisher, Mary Jane Nielsen, Vemmy Nielsen and Muffy Vrana contained nine versions of it. Astounding!

It's hard to pinpoint the Esquire Club's opening, but Lincoln newspapers began referencing the private supper club in 1958. The club, most likely owned then by J. Roland and Edna Francke and managed by their son, Jim, made its home at 960 Grand in West Lincoln.

When the village of West Lincoln was annexed by Lincoln on January 4, 1966, the Esquire's address changed to 960 West Cornhusker Highway. The private club remained in operation until April 1971, when the Franckes filed a voluntary bankruptcy petition.

The following March, J. Roland Francke reopened it as a public restaurant called the Esquire, dropping the word *club*, since membership was no longer required. The Esquire lasted just over a year, reopening at the end of May 1973 as Poor Arnold's.

But like a cat with nine lives, the Esquire was resilient.

According to the *Lincoln Journal*, it reopened in May 1975 in the same location at 960 West Cornhusker Highway, under the ownership of Leon and Carol Jurgensen and Bob and Polly Jurgensen. The restaurant sold sixteen-ounce broiled lobster tail dinners for $9.75 and received a "good lunch response to its businessman's steak, high-piled sandwiches and soups of the day."

The restaurant again closed in the fall of 1977 when the building was razed for Cornhusker Highway expansion. Larson transferred the eatery's liquor license to the nightclub Personalities Bandisco Lounge, then in the Haymarket at 826 P Street.

In April 1979, Larson brought back the Esquire Club once more, this time at 3235 South 13th Street in Indian Village. The restaurant still boasted the businessman's steak sandwich for lunch, but it was known for its steak and seafood, including, interestingly, frog legs served with lemon and tartar sauce. The restaurant lasted a year before giving way to Tucker's Inn on May 1, 1980.

Jim Francke, who had by then left Lincoln to manage restaurants in Los Angeles and Reno, Nevada, returned in 1991 and reopened the last iteration of the Esquire Club at 311 North Cotner Boulevard.

According to the *Lincoln Star*, the new restaurant featured a "comfortably elegant interior that borrows a bit of nostalgia from its predecessor. Black-and-white publicity stills of past Esquire entertainers occupy much of the wall space."

The dinner menu included steaks, prime rib, seafood, salads and sandwiches. Servers started evening guests with a relish tray full of crisp vegetables, pickled herring (another Esquire notable favorite), crackers and, you guessed it, the pink cream cheese beer dip.

Why red food coloring was added instead of any other color we'll never know. But pink is how people remember it—that and its horseradish flavor.

Francke operated the Esquire Club until the fall of 1995, when it closed for good. The restaurant held an auction of its equipment and furnishings in April 1996. The restaurant had lasted, off and on, for nearly forty years.

That cream cheese beer dip, however, will continue to live on forever.

Grandmother's

In April 1993, Applebee's opened in Lincoln at 3730 Village Drive in the Williamsburg neighborhood, but thanks to such places as Grandmother's, Lincoln diners already were familiar with the neighborhood restaurant concept.

In 1984, Grandmother's opened its second location at 70th and A Streets. Unlike its first store at 201 Sun Valley Boulevard, which sat in an industrialized area off of West O Street, the Grandmother's in east Lincoln found itself surrounded by residential homes, from which it drew many of its customers and employees.

"It was a great neighborhood bar," said Grandmother's longtime general manager Matt Smith. "When I was the bartender at Sun Valley Boulevard, I had so much fun bartending. It was such a great atmosphere for the employees and management. When I came over to 70th and A, I wanted to create that atmosphere for our employees, and I wanted it to be fun for our guests.

"You still had to execute. You had to have great food and great service. But I wanted to be a fun, neighborhood bar. I think that's what we ended up with."

All ages gathered at the east Lincoln Grandmother's. They came for the clam chowder and the fried chicken, for the Sunday buffets and Mexican Mondays and to sing karaoke on Wednesday and Saturday nights. They came before and after their sons' or daughters' events at nearby Lincoln East and Lincoln Pius X High Schools.

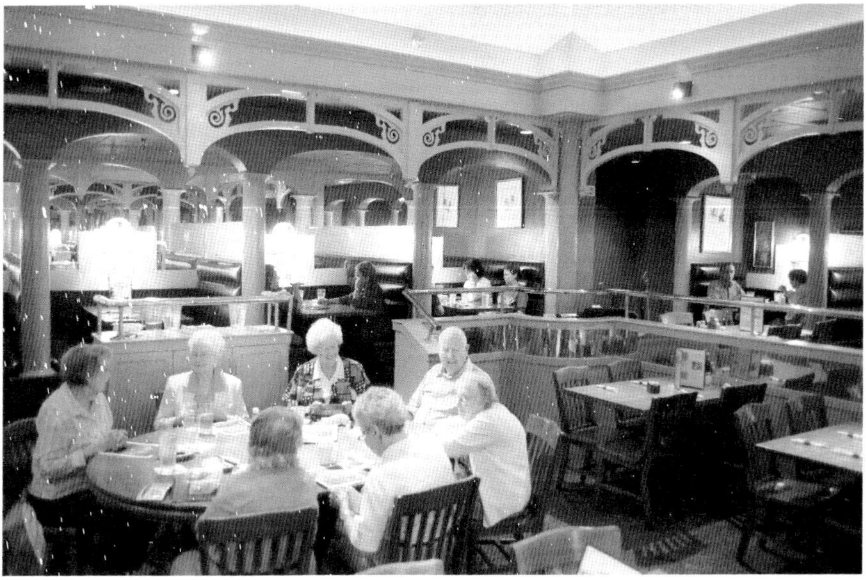

Diners enjoy a meal at Grandmother's in June 2008. *Courtesy of the* Lincoln Journal Star.

"You probably can't talk to a kid or a family that went to Lincoln East or Pius that weren't intimately acquainted with Grandmother's," Smith said. "Sporting events and the schools in general...we were great benefactors of them because they came out so much. And we got so many employees from them. The schools were great for us."

So when Grandmother's closed in February 2016, it was comparable to a death in the family for many of its loyal customers.

"I was stunned," Gina Grosenbach told the *Lincoln Journal Star* the day after Grandmother's closed. She and her husband, Dave, had dined at the restaurant often. She also worked there in the late 1980s. Her daughters, Megan and Makenna, had worked there, too.

"I loved their food," Gina told the newspaper. "Loved their staff. I'm still getting choked up that it's not going to be there anymore."

Lincoln resident J. Hoffman felt the same. He and his wife, Jamie, enjoyed their first date there in 1984 and celebrated their twenty-fifth wedding anniversary there in 2011. Two of their three children worked there.

"I bet we went there every couple of weeks," Hoffman told the *Journal Star*. "It was a Saturday highlight for us."

Dean Rasmussen, whose restaurant résumé includes King's Food Host, and his brother-in-law Bob Kerrey, who eventually became Nebraska governor, U.S. senator and presidential candidate, opened the first Grandmother's in Ralston in 1973. They brought the concept to Lincoln, opening Grandmother's Skillet on Sun Valley Boulevard in December 1976. The investors included Rasmussen, Kerrey, John Goff, Dion Bennett and Dennis Sullivan.

The restaurant prided itself on its home-style menu, with many of its made-from-scratch entrees prepared from Kerrey's mother's recipes. Grandmother's hand-pattied its hamburgers and hand-breaded its onion rings.

Lincoln's original Grandmother's changed its name to Kerrey's in 1988, when Goff broke off from the original investment group to create Creative Foods Inc. with Rasmussen and Kerrey as limited partners. Big Red Keno Ltd. purchased Kerrey's in 1994.

Matt Smith began working at Grandmother's in Lincoln in October 1981 and entered the store's management training program in 1982. The second Grandmother's opened in February 1984, with Smith taking over as general manager in May 1985. The new store was nearly eight thousand square feet, with a large bar area and a dining room with booth and table seating.

"John [Goff] was very good at promotion," Smith said. "He did things like [having] penny meal days, where a meal would cost you a penny. It was unbelievably busy. People would experience [Grandmother's]. We lost money, but as as a promotional tool, it was phenomenal. John did all sorts of things."

Such as all-you-could-eat barbecue ribs.

"We called them Western Days," Smith said. "It was a two-week deal. The barbecue ribs and corn-on-the-cob were all you can eat for a set price. Now, everybody and their dog does an all-you-can-eat-type thing. But now all-you-can-eat doesn't hold the same type of allure as it used to as people eat less. Back then, all-you-can-eat was a big deal."

Grandmother's thrived in 1990s and early 2000s. During its heyday, the store at 70th and A was full every night, busy enough to warrant 110 to 120 employees and 5 managers. The recession in the late 2000s and increased competition took their toll, Smith said. Rasmussen, meanwhile, had found success with the fast-casual concept of Don & Millie's, with seven stores operating in Omaha and Lincoln.

After the original store in Ralston closed in 2014, the Lincoln location was the last Grandmother's operating in Nebraska. Today, a sports bar operates at the site.

"It's been a tremendous ride," Smith told the *Journal Star* in 2016. "We are greatly indebted to the community."

Grandmother's French Onion Soup

2¼ pounds onions, diced
1 ounce margarine
3 tablespoons beef base
2 teaspoons chicken base
1 quart hot water
3 tablespoons sherry
Black pepper, pinch
2½ quarts water
Croutons
Provolone cheese

Sauté onion in margarine for 5–10 minutes or until soft. In a soup kettle, dissolve beef and chicken base in hot water. Add onions. Stir in sherry, pepper and water. Bring to a boil, turn down heat and simmer covered for 25 minutes. To serve, fill soup bowl with 8 ounces of hot soup, add croutons to cover soup and top with 1 ounce of provolone cheese. Melt cheese in a broiler until desired doneness. Makes 1 gallon.

—Courtesy of Matt Smith, Grandmother's

Jax Shack

"The former Jax Shack has become the 'Love Shack.'" That's how I had started my review for the *Lincoln Journal Star* in March 2001 regarding the southeast Lincoln restaurant and referencing the title of a popular hit of new wave band the B-52's.

Already known as one of Lincoln's top places to eat, Jax Restaurant & Lounge at 27th Street and Woods Boulevard had become *the* place to get engaged.

Manager David Barr estimated two or three marriage proposals occurred each month at the restaurant. Grooms-to-be called ahead and arranged the special moment and often requested the restaurant's alcove, which provided intimacy and privacy.

"We'll hide the ring on the dessert tray or present it with a dessert or with flowers," Barr told me. "All sorts of ways."

With its tasteful décor, top-notch menu and attentive, polite servers, for years, Jax proved to be the perfect place for the first date, fiftieth anniversary celebration or even everyday occasions.

It had been that way since Emmy Lou and John Mettlen opened Jax Shack in 1977 and continued after Lincoln investor Dale Jensen bought it in 1994 and dropped Shack from the name.

The Mettlens patterned their restaurant after German pubs, or *Ratskeller*, they saw during a European trip in 1976, featuring multiple levels and exposed brick. The restaurant had comfortable booths in a maroon and hunter paisley motif and solid, dark wood tables and chairs. The best dining spot, other than the alcove, was near the fireplace, which provided some additional ambiance.

"I didn't want people to feel they were eating in a shopping center, and I wanted to give customers the sensation that they had been transported far away," Emmy Lou told the *Lincoln Star in* 1983.

The menu contained selections of beef, chicken, seafood and pasta dishes. The restaurant, keeping with its "love" theme also offered a number of decadent desserts—good places to hide a ring.

Sadly, the restaurant closed in July 2001, just a few months after my review, citing a decline in business. "We're sad to see it go," Barr told the *Lincoln Journal Star*. "We would like to see it go on. Over the last few years in this part of town a lot of new franchises have started. It's very hard for independent operations."

Still, Jax provided many couples with memories they will never forget.

Jax Shack's English Trifle

Jax Shack used a version devised by Billie Oakley, a former radio and TV personality in Iowa, South Dakota and Nebraska, including Lincoln's KOLN/KGIN-TV, who died in 1996 at the age of seventy-eight.

1 small box vanilla pudding, instant or regular
10 ounces pound cake
Small jar strawberry preserves
Small package halved frozen strawberries
2 ounces brandy
½ pint whipping cream
Maraschino cherries
Parsley

Prepare pudding as directed. Cover bottom of 7-by-11-by-2-inch pan with pound cake cut into ½-inch squares. Layer with preserves, creating another ¼-inch layer. Thaw strawberries and place over the preserves, creating another ¼-inch layer. Drizzle evenly with brandy (amount may be decreased or increased according to taste). Pour cool pudding over cake. Cover and chill at least four hours or overnight. Whip cream. Place chilled cake mixture into stemmed sherbet glasses or fluted champagne glasses, taking care to keep cake in respective layers. Top serving with whipped cream. Add cherry and parsley sprig on top. Serves 6 to 8.

—Chef's Corner, *Lincoln Star*, July 27, 1983

K's Restaurant

The Lincoln mayor couldn't see what was happening. She was too short. So a determined Helen Boosalis climbed atop a chair and then a table to witness the filming of the Academy Award–winning *Terms of Endearment* at K's Restaurant.

"She really wanted to see the movie being made," owner Kay Brestel said. "It was so funny."

K's may be the only restaurant in Lincoln to appear in a major motion picture. It's surely the only one from the city to appear in a film that won an Oscar for Best Picture.

Paramount Pictures filmed *Terms of Endearment* at several Lincoln locations in the spring of 1983, including K's.

At the time, Brestel served on the Lincoln Economic Development Commission, so she knew Paramount was looking at properties in the city. But she never dreamed hers would be one of them.

"When the phone rang, it was the director of the film company," Brestel remembered. "I thought somebody was pulling my leg. He wanted to know if it was OK to let the scouts come in and take a look around. They wanted something that looked like a Norman Rockwell picture, and we were perfect with the antiques, curtains and wood."

K's not only became a film site but also a place for Nebraska governor Bob Kerrey and star Debra Winger to meet up later for a date. Their subsequent romance made headlines.

"It's fun to go back and remember all these little things," Brestel said. "They ate in a tiny room at the back, in a nook. He would bring her in the evenings. It was very private. He loved my menu. They would wine and dine in the evenings after the the movie was made."

Terms of Endearment earned eleven Academy Award nominations in 1984 and won five, including for stars Shirley MacLaine (best actress), Jack Nicholson (supporting actor) and director James L. Brooks. The movie also put K's Restaurant on the map.

"It was the best advertising in the world," Brestel said. Not that K's needed much help.

In the early 1970s, when Brestel's three children were old enough for school, she began waiting tables at Scott's Pancake Shoppe in the Piedmont Shopping Center at 1275 South Cotner Boulevard. After three months, owner Bob Scott promoted her to hostess, then to manager.

In 1977, Scott, who had opened a downtown store, offered to sell Brestel the Piedmont restaurant if she agreed to run it as a Scott's for a year before changing the name to K's Restaurant. Brestel acquired a $50,000 bank loan to do so.

"It was a miracle that I could get it," Brestel said. "He let me, on my signature [alone], borrow money for the payment of the restaurant. So that was pretty incredible."

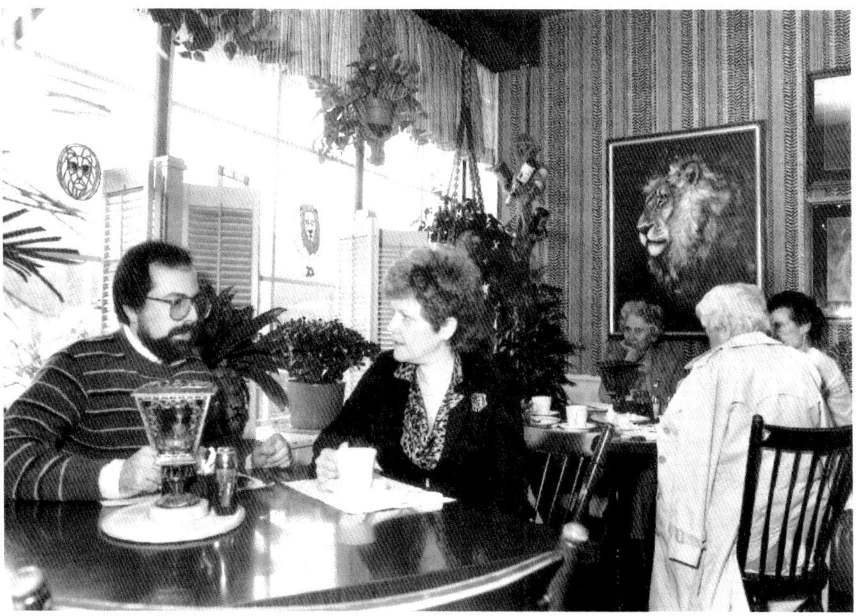

K's Restaurant owner Kay Brestel (*right*) meets with director James L. Brooks in April 1983 to discuss the restaurant as a site for filming *Terms of Endearment*. *Courtesy of the* Lincoln Journal Star.

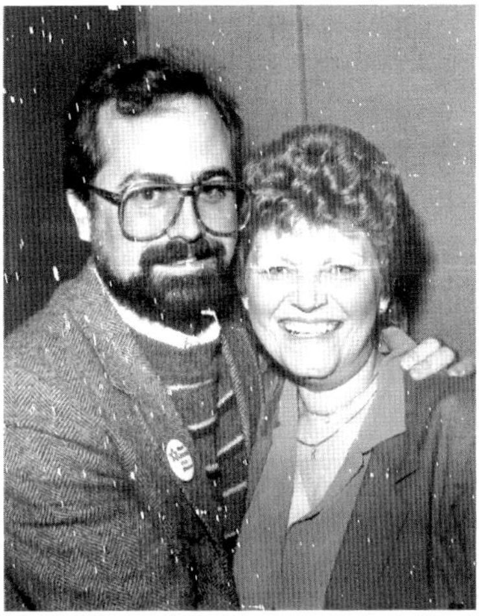

K's Restaurant owner poses with *Terms of Endearment* director James L. Brooks. Brooks filmed scenes of the Academy Award winner at K's in 1983. *Courtesy of Beth Haase.*

She went to work—day and night—to succeed, cooking, waiting and bussing tables and cleaning. She never took a salary. And in five years, she paid off the loan, never borrowing again or taking any investors. Her work was noticed: in 1991, the Horizons Chapter of the American Business Women's Association awarded Brestel its Outstanding Business Woman Award.

Scott's Pancake Shoppe had served breakfast fare only. K's built from there, adding a lunch and dinner entrées. The restaurant quickly became known for its fresh-baked breads, homemade soups, all-day breakfast, more than twenty burgers and sandwiches and dinner entrées ranging from assorted seafood, beef, chicken, pork and pasta.

In 1994, a *Lincoln Journal* reviewer claimed that K's offered the best salmon steak in Lincoln, serving it with garlic-lemon butter or, as the Friday night special, with a creamy béarnaise sauce.

The restaurant featured an Americana theme (hence, the Normal Rockwell comparison) with walnut wood tables and antique clocks.

"I never wanted to change that," Brestel said. "That was a very homespun-type atmosphere. When I built that other room—I'm a Leo birthday—and at that time, I had a dear friend that traveled to Africa all the time. He was a photographer and collector of items. He would go on trips and bring me back all kind of [lion] artifacts. I had all kinds of [lion] things to decorate."

Brestel named the adjoining dining area the Simba Room, and it contained lion items numbering in the hundreds. The menu cover featured a Neal Anderson drawing of the King of Beasts.

"Over the years, every time I would see a lion picture or something to do with lions I would buy it," Brestel said. "By the time, I got out of here, I had lots and lots of lions to give away. I was purebred Leo, and I went off on that for some reason. It was very effective. Everybody loved that room. They had to go eat in there."

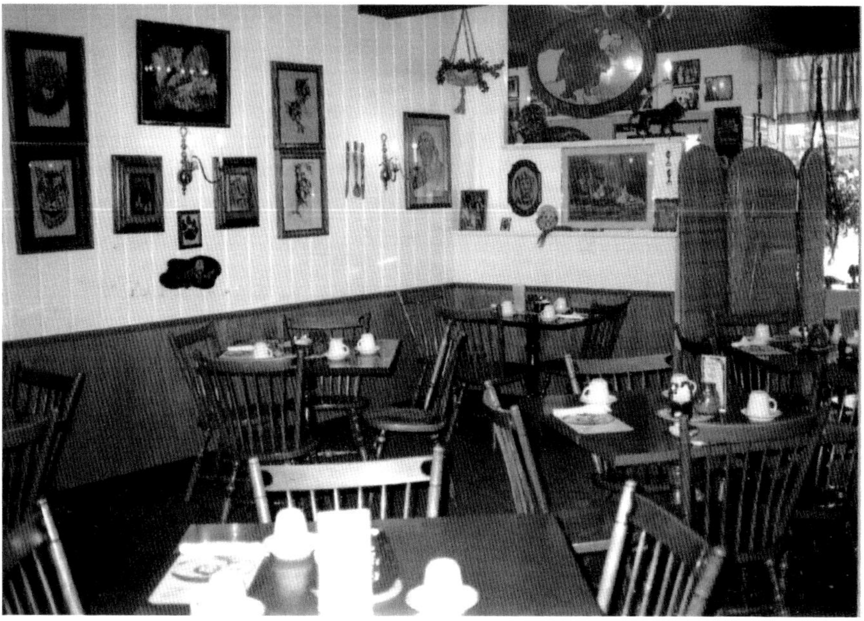

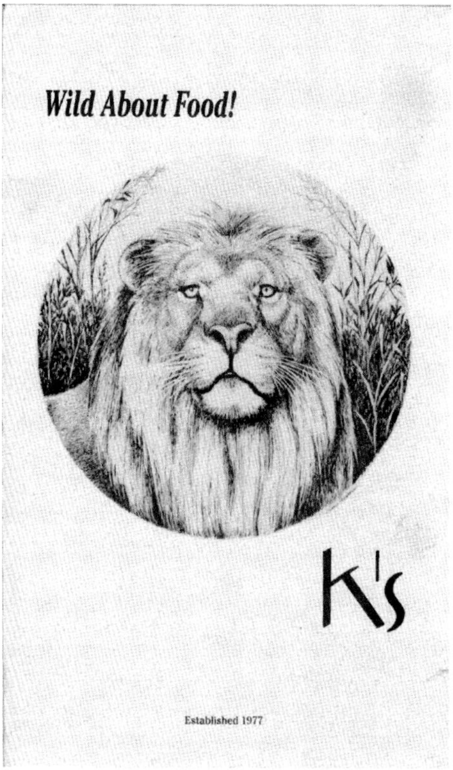

Above: The Simba Room at K's Restaurant was decorated in a lion motif and was a favorite of the customers. *Courtesy of Beth Haase.*

Left: The K's Restaurant menu included a drawing of a lion, which was the décor motif. *Courtesy of Beth Haase.*

K's also offered live music in the Simba Room. On weekends, local musician Paul Burner parked himself on a stool with his guitar in front of the fireplace and serenade diners with oldies and originals.

In 1980, the *Lincoln Journal* touted K's as one of two Lincoln restaurants offering low-calorie entrées. The menu's "skinny gourmet," à la carte items included a six-ounce broiled chicken breast, baked halibut, broiled lean chuck beef, salads and stir-fried vegetables cooked in a wok without oil.

A few years later, according to Brestel, K's became the first to introduce American Heart Association–endorsed heart-healthy meals. In February 1985, Nebraska football coach Tom Osborne suffered a heart attack and was hospitalized at nearby Bryan Hospital, which had developed a relationship with Brestel.

"Well, after [Osborne] had his surgery, one of the first places he came to eat was K's," Brestel remembered. "I even ordered buffalo meat from a Nebraska rancher so you could have pure ground meat that you could eat."

K's proved to be a family affair. All three Brestel children—Brad, Beth and Brenda—worked at the restaurant. Brad was executive chef and general manager. Beth was part-owner and general manager when they decided to put the restaurant on the market in 1995. She sold it in 1996. It continued as K's under different owners into the early 2000s, when it closed for good. Today, the Piedmont Bistro by Venue operates in K's location.

K's Oreo Cheesecake

Oreo Crust

2 cups Oreo crumbs
¼ cup sugar
½ cup melted margarine

Cheesecake Batter

2 pounds cream cheese
1 ¼ cups sugar
4 eggs
½ tablespoon vanilla
1 ½ cups chopped Oreo cookies

Sour Cream Topping

2 cups sour cream

¼ cup sugar
½ teaspoon vanilla

Ganache Topping
2 cups chocolate chips
1 cup cream
1 teaspoon vanilla
Oreo cookies, for garnish

Combine crust ingredients and press evenly on bottom of springform pan. Gradually cream cheese until soft. Beat in sugar; add eggs one at a time and vanilla. Pour ¼ cheesecake batter into the springform pan. Chop up 1½ cups of Oreo cookies and spread on top of batter. Pour rest of the batter on top of the Oreos. Cover pan with foil and put the springform pan into a larger pan with hot water. Bake at 350 degrees for 15 minutes. Lower oven temperature to 325 degrees and bake for about 60 minutes. It will be done when internal temperature is 165 degrees. While baking, combine ingredients for sour cream topping. Remove from oven and top with sour cream topping. Bake another 10 minutes at 325 degrees. Remove from oven and cool. Then put in refrigerator to continue cooling. When cooled, take off spring side. You also may cool in freezer. Once cooled, combine ingredients for ganache topping and slowly microwave, stirring frequently. When mixture is smooth, pour over cake. Separate 8 Oreo cookies into 16 half pieces. Decorate top of cake by putting Oreo cookies halves on top of cake for each slice. Put in refrigerator to let ganache harden.

—Courtesy of Beth Haase, K's Restaurant

K's Restaurant Chicken Supreme Soup

This homemade soup was served on Sundays at K's; Brestel said some customers came in specifically for it.

¾ cup chopped onion
1 cup grated carrot
¾ cup chopped fresh mushrooms

1 ½ cups chopped celery
¼ cup butter
3 cups chopped chicken or turkey
½ teaspoon celery seed
Pinch of sage
Pinch of thyme
1 bay leaf
1 tablespoon tamari or soy sauce
1 tablespoon parsley flakes
1 teaspoon basil
2 tablespoons red wine
2 quarts water or soup stock
½ cup butter
¾ cup white flour

Saute onion, carrot, mushrooms and celery in butter until tender. Add chicken, celery seed, sage, thyme, bay leaf tamari, parsley flakes, basil and wine and let cook for 10 to 15 minutes. Then add water or soup stock and bring to a boil. Cook a roux of the butter and flour. Add to the soup mixture and stir until thick. Serves about five people.

—Chef's Corner, the *Lincoln Star*, May 16, 1984

The Knolls Restaurant

For more than fifty years, the restaurant at the Knolls Golf Club was open to the public. The trouble was not everybody knew it.

George Boosalis, whose family had owned the restaurant since 1966, heard it more than once over the years.

In 1984, the *Lincoln Star* noted the Knolls's identity problem in a restaurant review. Membership was required to swim, golf and play tennis at the club but not to eat.

"We've had people who've lived in town for eight years say, 'Oh, I thought you were private,'" Boosalis told the newspaper.

In June 2001, when I reviewed the restaurant for the *Journal Star*, I noted the same thing, writing that "though it's been around for almost 35 years, some people still don't know The Knolls is open to the public. And, until recently, I was one of those people, even though I'm a born-and-raised Lincolnite."

"It's a stigma my dad has had from the beginning," Boosalis told me for my story. "The restaurant is public, but the club is private. It's how we're able to keep membership dues reasonable."

But those who did know about Lincoln's best-kept secret enjoyed some incredible food. The Knolls, under the Boosalis family leadership, was home to arguably the city's best buffet, which always featured a carving table. I can still taste the prime rib from it. The club also had menu service, which complemented the buffet nicely.

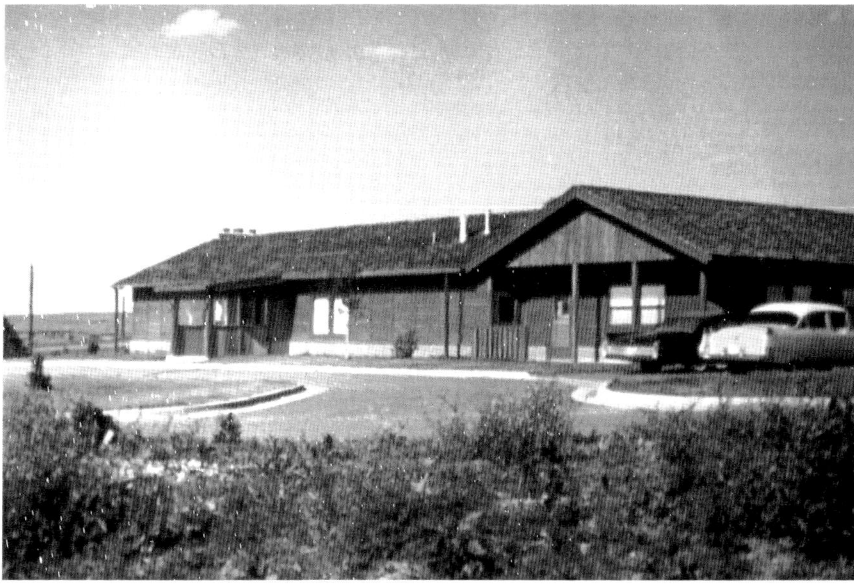

The Knolls Country Club opened its golf course in 1963 and the restaurant three years later. While the club was private, the restaurant was open to the public and became known for its buffet. *Courtesy of Jim McKee.*

Interestingly, folks in Lincoln began eating at the Knolls before they began playing golf there.

In May 1963, the new par-3 golf club introduced a Chef Crosby in a newspaper ad, saying its restaurant was now open and serving "buffet style." The club also noted in the ad that it was air conditioned.

Two months later, the course—"one mile south and [a] half mile east of the penitentiary"—opened for business, with a restaurant, "famous for fine foods," operating from 7:00 a.m. to 9:30 a.m. Tuesday–Sunday and from 7:00 a.m. to 2:00 p.m. on Monday. The restaurant featured indoor and patio dining. By the end of the year, the restaurant had new chef, Frank Dunham.

In August 1966, a new group, which included John Boosalis as a partner, purchased the golf course. Three months later, the Knolls began advertising for its "all new restaurant now open to the public." It featured a $1.25 continental buffet from 11:30 a.m. to 2:00 p.m. on Mondays. A regular buffet with prime rib, barbecue ribs, pan-fried chicken, ham and trout filets ran nightly and Sundays and cost $2.25.

The Boosalis family continued to run the Knolls until October 2015, when it sold the golf course and restaurant. An Omaha real estate company redeveloped part of the land into a retirement community.

John Boosalis turned the Knolls over to his sons Gregg and George in 1981. Gregg left the business in 1990. In 1967, the course became private, but the restaurant remained open to the public.

Right up to the end, the Knolls maintained its buffet service, often drawing raves from dining critics and diners alike. "It was a great run," George Boosalis told the *Journal Star* on the club's auction day.

The Knolls's Beef Tips Burgundy

Don Schwarz, the Knolls chef who devised the recipe, recommended the beef tips be served over brown or white rice.

1 ½ pounds sirloin steak
½ teaspoon garlic powder
½ teaspoon onion salt
½ teaspoon season salt
4 cups beef stock or bouillon
2 tablespoons butter
1 onion, finely chopped
1 green pepper, medium chopped
¼ pound fresh mushrooms, sliced
¼ cup red burgundy wine
1 to 1 ½ tablespoons flour
Salt and pepper, to taste

Trim the steak and cut it into 1-inch cubes. Brown cubes evenly on all sides in a large pot or skillet. Add all seasonings. Add beef stock or bouillon. Cover and simmer until steak is tender (about one hour). Heat butter in a second pan and sauté onions, green peppers and mushrooms over low heat until soft and just beginning to color. Drain off butter. After steak is tender, add vegetables and wine. Mix drained butter and flour together for a roux. Blend together until smooth. Add to beef burgundy until desired thickness and let simmer for about 20 minutes. Serve over rice. Serves four.

—Chef's Corner, the *Lincoln Star*, October 10, 1984

Legionnaire Club

The 1978 Nebraska-Oklahoma football game is remembered by Cornhusker fans for many reasons, from OU's Billy Sims's fumble at the three-yard line and NU's John Ruud's crushing hit of Kelly Phelps on a kickoff to Nebraska coach Tom Osborne finally beating his nemesis after five straight losses.

But what happened after the game is what sticks with Rob Logsdon.

Then just twenty-one years old, Rob worked alongside his father, Bob Logsdon, who ran the Legionnaire Club. The private social and dining operation affiliated with Lincoln's American Legion Post 3 was the city's hottest nightspot.

And when Osborne walked through the club's door…

"Women were standing on the tables," Rob Logsdon said. "I'm like 'Do you want me to get them down, Dad?' He goes 'No, just let 'em go.' The place just erupted when Osborne walked in."

According to the *Lincoln Journal-Star*, the scene bore striking similarities to one in the early 1960s when the Husker football team, under coach Bob Devaney, won the the Big 8 conference title.

"I forget what year," Bob Logsdon told the paper. "The coaches used to have a party room in the basement. They came upstairs, and everybody in that place was on the tables cheering. It just about brought tears to my eyes. I remember people by the hundreds, Legionnaires from outstate, came because they heard the coaches were out there after games."

Indeed they did.

Bob Logsdon and Devaney were close, with Logsdon serving as a pallbearer at Devaney's funeral in 1997.

"They just really hit it off," Rob Logsdon said. "They were just great friends. Bob and [wife] Phyllis would come out quite often. [Lincoln)] would get a lot of players' families from out of town, and the families would come to the Legion. So you would see a lot of the players there, too."

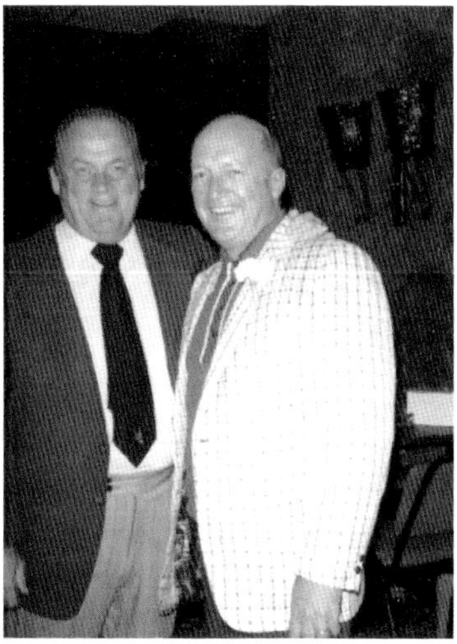

Nebraska athletic director Bob Devaney (*left*) poses for a photo in September 1972 with Legionnaire Club general manager Bob Logsdon inside the club. *Courtesy of Rob Logsdon.*

The friendship led to an off-site contract between the Legion and Nebraska's athletic department. Rob said his dad overheard Devaney asking assistants Monte Kiffin and Warren Powers "whose turn it was to get the sandwiches" for their regular Sunday afternoon film session and game-planning.

"Dad was like 'I'll feed you. How many of you are there?'" Rob Logsdon said. "That started a twenty-five-year run of dad feeding the football coaches in their offices at five o'clock every Sunday. When Devaney became athletic director and came out to the club, I would drive Dad and Devaney down to feed the coaches on Sunday nights. Dad did that all through the Osborne era and most of the [Frank] Solich era."

A certain college football TV announcer was known to dine at the Legion. The late Keith Jackson, a Marine Corps veteran who many regarded as the voice of college football, was a guest of Devaney's, who had become Nebraska's athletic director after the 1972 season.

"I still remember Devaney and Keith Jackson one Friday night before the Nebraska-Oklahoma game, and Dad sat me down and said 'You have to listen to this,'" Rob Logsdon said. "The stories that Devaney and Keith Jackson started telling....I mean I truly wish I could have recorded it because the two men were just hilarious. Devaney telling his stories...he was a funny man."

Lincoln's American Legion Post 3 was organized in 1919 following World War I. In 1955, it moved from the Lincoln Hotel to 1525 P Street. Bob Logsdon, who had previously owned the Spigot in downtown Lincoln, took over as the Legion Club's general manager in 1958, overseeing its move

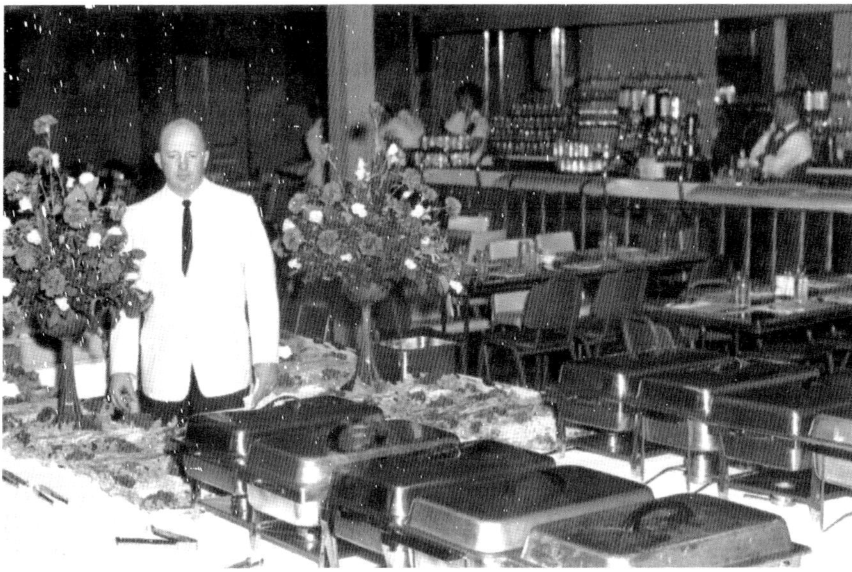

Bob Logsdon surveys a buffet setup in the Legionnaire Club sometime in the 1960s. *Courtesy of Rob Logsdon.*

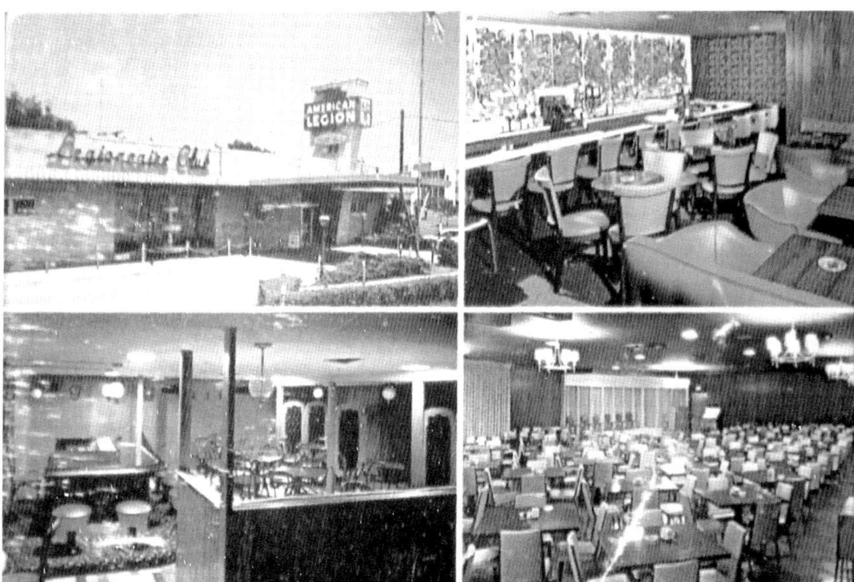

The postcard shows three interior shots, including a very retro-looking lounge, top right, and an exterior of the Legionnaire Club at 5730 O Street. *Courtesy of Jim McKee.*

in June 1960 when it purchased Tony Domino's Italian Village at 5730 O Street for $185,000.

That's when the club began to come into its own, becoming a nightlife choice for World War II and Korean War veterans and their wives.

"When they say that was the Greatest Generation, it truly was," Rob Logsdon said. "People would be out there during the week, and they would come back on weekends, a table of six or eight of them, and they knew how to live."

In 1962, five-year-old Rob Logsdon would head to the Legionnaire Club after kindergarten to join his father, setting up the tables before the dinner rush.

"That took a five-year-old some time because the dining room was four hundred seats," he said. "My father paid me a quarter an hour out of his pocket."

Later, Bob Logsdon had the youngster "work" the door.

"They propped me up on a stool at the entrance," Rob Logsdon said. "You had to be buzzed in and show your membership card. Well, me, who could barely read, I would just nod at the membership cards."

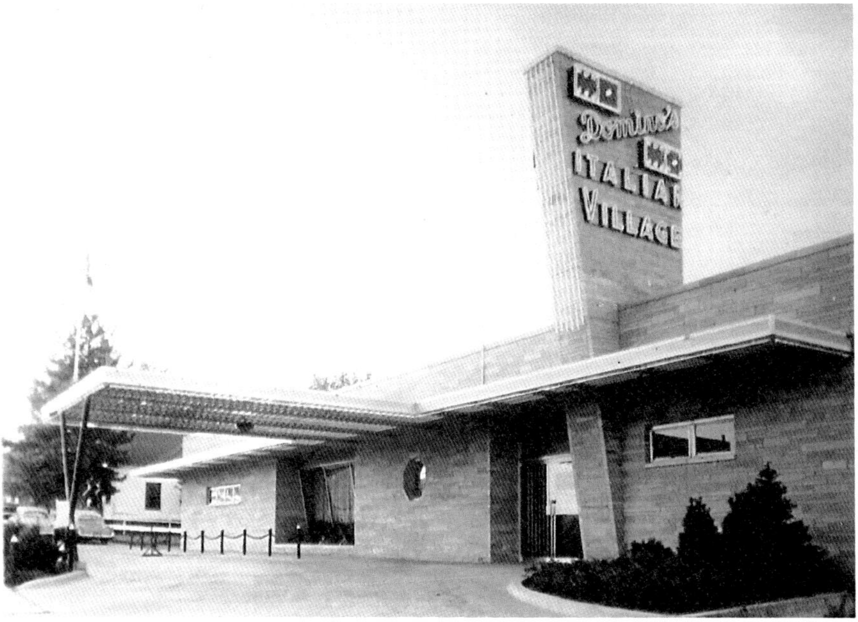

Before being sold to American Legion Post 3, the building at 5730 O Street was home to Domino's Italian Village. *Courtesy of Jim McKee.*

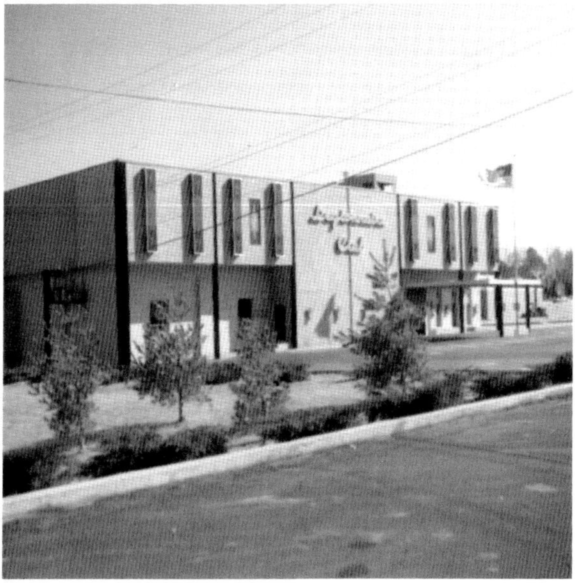

The Legionnaire Club moved in 1960 from downtown to 5730 O Street and later added a second floor, as seen here. *Courtesy of Rob Logsdon.*

Rob Logsdon worked off and on—"It was how I got to spend time with Dad"—until Bob Logsdon left the club in the mid-1990s. Bob went to become chairman of the state Liquor Control Commission and died in 2012. Rob Logsdon witnessed the club's popularity during its peak years in the 1960s, '70s and '80s. There were three kitchens and multiple dining areas with names such as "submarine," "state" and "board" rooms.

Steak—New York strips, ribeyes and filets and sometime porterhouses and T-bones—was the meal of choice, served with salad, soup, potato and a dinner roll. Dinner started with a hunk of cheddar on a cheese board and a basket of crackers.

Evenings included live entertainment—no cover charge. The Turpin Family Band regularly performed, as did jazz/blues pianist Jay McShann from Kansas City, Missouri.

The place was crazy busy. Saturday nights during the football season saw the dining room turning over as many as six times, feeding up to 1,800 to 1,900 people.

"We had several years we did $2 million in business," Bob Logsdon told the *Lincoln Journal Star* in 2002. "And the food check average was not $7, and we were only open at night."

In 1997, the club moved once more, to 5630 P Street, and sold its building for $1.1 million. But it would make it only another five years, closing in August 2002 because the club was losing too much money, according to then

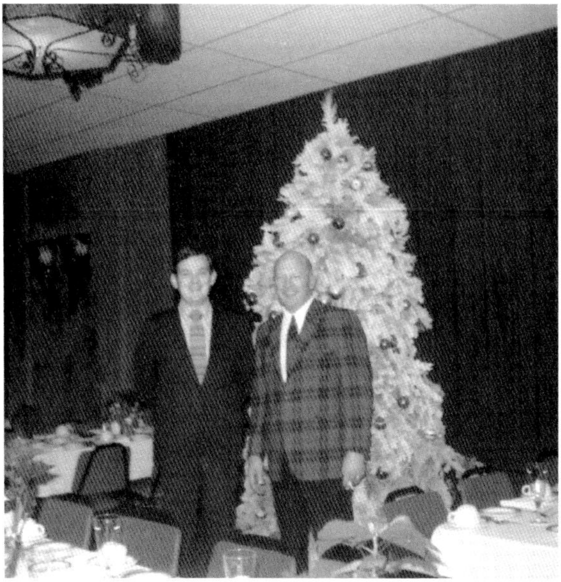

Stu Jordal (*left*) and Bob Logsdon pose for a photo in December 1970 inside the Legionnaire Club. *Courtesy of Rob Logsdon.*

president Ralph King. The reason was obvious: its old clientele was dying off and new veterans weren't joining.

"The last time I ate at the Legion club on P Street, it was really kind of sad because you would see tables of four people and it would be one guy and three women and you knew two of those women were widows," Rob Logsdon said. "That used to a six-top that would be coming to eat at the club all the time. That's where it changed."

Still, for a time, there was no place quite like the Legionnaire Club in Lincoln.

"It was a perfect place at a perfect time, when all the stars kind of aligned," Rob Logsdon said. "There weren't that many places to go, and there was such a bond with these veterans. It was a true gathering place."

Lincoln Exchange

The Lincoln Exchange may be remembered as much for its location as for its food.

Opened in October 1980, the restaurant occupied the first floors of the adjoining historic Nebraska Telephone Company and Woods Brothers Buildings at 130 and 132 South 13th Streets, respectively.

Thomas Rogers Kimball of the architectural firm Walker and Kimball designed the telephone building in the Renaissance Revival style in 1894. Occupied in 1896, it was probably the first building erected as a telephone exchange in Lincoln.

The Woods building, designed in 1914 by the Woods Brothers Construction Company and completed in 1916, incorporates Neoclassical Revival elements.

The buildings were what drew Frank Hardin and Tamas Allan. Motif restaurants were in vogue in the late 1970s and early '80s. Hardin already co-owned and operated the Lincoln Underground in another old Lincoln building.

Using a historic site "immediately gives you the atmosphere, and with an easier, more comfortable level of acceptance than some motif set up with props and assembly-line fake antiques and curios," Hardin said in October 1980 in a special commemorative issue of the *Exchange*.

"Lincoln has a lot of really unique-looking buildings," Hardin said. "We've all become glass and steel. And, we need a little bit of brick and mortar, plus the more ornate the design of another, to remind us of what thing are and what our heritage is."

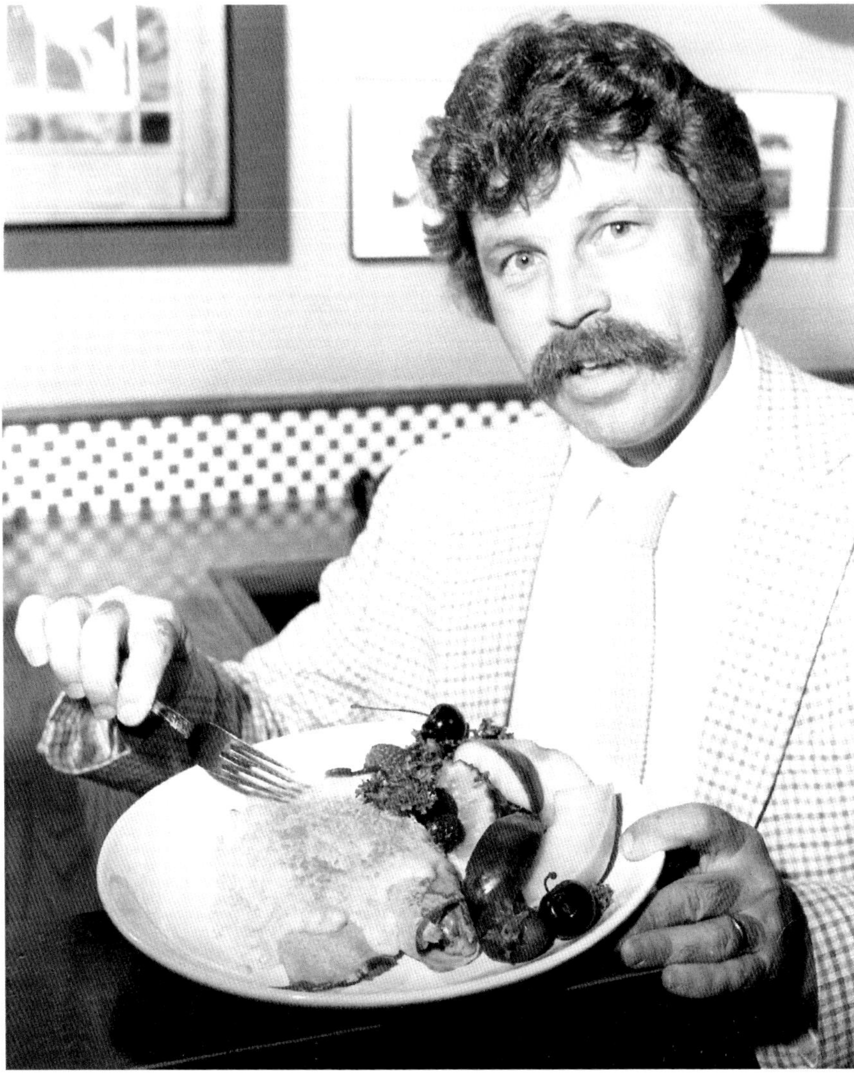

Frank Hardin, who at one point had a hand in the Lincoln Underground and Lincoln Exchange, shows off the Exchange's Crepe Neptune in August 1983. *Courtesy of the* Lincoln Journal Star.

With the Lincoln Exchange, Hardin and Allan created a fine-dining experience in Lincoln. Inside, the restaurant featured red carpet, a stained-glass chandelier and an oak bar decorated with 350 pieces of beveled glass.

Patterned after French bistros, the lunch menu included sandwiches, quiches, pastas and omelets. Dinners were, of course, more elaborate, with duck, beef, chicken and seafood selections. The Exchange, at the time, was Lincoln's go-to place for seafood.

"A lot of big bankers and stockbrokers, lawyers and CPAs who work in this area kind of consider this their local pub," manager Herb Thomas told the *Lincoln Star* in 1985.

In addition to Thomas, who later managed the Rotisserie/Grotto for a number of years, the Exchange employed several others who became known on Lincoln's dining scene, most notably Nader Farahbod, who would go on to open Billy's in 1986.

The restaurant, however, wasn't without its financial troubles. It changed ownership in 1984 and closed for five weeks in the summer of 1985 for "renovation and reorganization." It closed in October 1986.

Lincoln Exchange's Crepe Neptune

Crepes
1 cup chicken stock
3 cups milk
1 tablespoon sherry
4 tablespoons flour
4 tablespoons butter
1 ½ cups grated Romano cheese
½ cup grated Parmesan cheese
½ cup chopped green onions or chives
¼ teaspoon garlic powder
½ teaspoon white pepper
Boiling water to cover seafood
Dash of white wine
½ lemon
Bay leaf
Dash of chopped parsley
10 ounces each scallops, shrimp, Alaska crab, cod filet or other whitefish
½ cup sliced mushrooms

Prepare or thaw enough crepes to use two per serving. Bring chicken stock, milk and sherry almost to a boil, but do not boil. Meanwhile, prepare a roux by stirring flour into melted butter heated to the frothy stage. Over medium heat, slowly add flour and stir until mixture forms a paste and has absorbed the butter. Add roux, a little at a time, to the hot stock and milk mixture, stirring continuously until mixture coats the spoon. Add cheeses, onion or chives, garlic and white pepper. Remove from heat and set aside.

Put enough water in large pan to cover the fish; add wine, lemon, bay leaf and parsley and bring to a boil. Add the scallops and whitefish; when water returns to a boil, add shrimp and crab. Boil a few minutes until the whitefish flakes easily. Don't overcook. Drain and discard the bouillon.

Lay two crepes side by side, overlapping no more than half; pour on small amount of sauce. Divide fish into six or eight equal portions; put whitefish first, then crab on crepes; surround fish and crab with scallops and cover with shrimp. Sprinkle with mushrooms and pour on a little more sauce. Roll sides of the crepes over to seal, cover with the remaining sauce and sprinkle with more Parmesan.

Bake at 350 degrees about 10 minutes or until bubbling. Then, watching carefully, brown under broiler. Serve immediately with fresh fruit or garden salad.

—Chef's Corner, the *Lincoln Star*, August 3, 1983

Lincoln Underground/Brittany's

People told Frank Hardin he was crazy to try to turn what many considered a hole in the ground into a restaurant. But Hardin had a vision, and what he saw was fine dining in a room a to remember.

Hardin transformed what the *Lincoln Journal* had called "part boiler room, part swamp and part storeroom" into the Lincoln Underground. It opened in October 1976 in the lower level at 227 North Ninth Street.

"Basically we cleaned everything up," he told the newspaper in 1976.

Did he ever.

At the turn of the twentieth century, the space was home to Lincoln Pure Butter Co. But Hardin's touch turned the room into something special. Hardin, who was part of an investment group that included Colorado businessmen, retained the original thick limestone walls. He dug up the floor and had plumbing installed. The new décor featured wood, exposed stone and brightly painted pipes in a motif Hardin called "Central European" — similar to something he had seen in then Czechoslovakia.

The restaurant seated 130 in three dining rooms and 50 more in the bar.

Hardin described the menu as "strictly American to Continental—from Rocky Mountain trout to Chateaubriand." It featured a mix of seafood, beef, veal and lamb. The Underground prepared some dishes and desserts tableside for added effect.

"We wanted to be something very special to Lincoln, so we adapted the whole thing to the basement," said Hardin, who four years later would help to open the Lincoln Exchange, another memorable Lincoln eatery.

The Underground was special until it wasn't. The restaurant, despite its attraction and what the *Lincoln Journal* called "one of the best restaurant ideas in Lincoln in years," lasted just over five years, closing in May 1983 with management buying a newspaper ad at the end of that month to thank Lincoln for its patronage.

In the spring of 1983, Lincolnite Tom Bittinger headed a partnership that planned a $750,000 development of the three-story, one-hundred-plus-year-old building, commonly referred to as the Lincoln Underground building, according to the *Lincoln Star*. Plans called for remodeling the main and lower levels into a new restaurant.

In September 1983, the Victorian-style Brittany's welcomed its first customers. It featured two lounges, first-floor dining and a historic bar. With its onyx insets, the bar was believed to have originated in the 1880s in the Bowery of San Francisco. For several years, it made its home at the Hob Nob on the north side of N Street between 11th and 12th Streets.

Ownership decorated the restaurant in deep green, burgundy and rose tones. It included authentic Victorian wall sconces, lighting fixtures, antique furnishings in the lobby area, stained glass, mirrors, brass railings and oils, prints and lithographs. The menu was international, to reflect its Victorian influence.

"I liked the Victorian decor," Bittinger told the *Lincoln Star* prior to the restaurant's opening. And combined with its location in the up-and-coming Haymarket district and the Hob Nob bar, "it all came together," Bittinger said.

Brittany's had a good run, lasting seven-plus years before closing on December 26, 1990. Just a few months before shutting down, the restaurant renamed its downstairs dining room the Underground, featuring a menu with dishes from the old Lincoln Underground prepared by Charles Speers, who was one of the Underground's original cooks.

In early 1991, Lincoln restaurateur Waheed Malik, then co-owner of the Oven in the Haymarket, reopened the lower level as—you guessed it—the Lincoln Underground, with Speer as executive chef. Malik told the *Lincoln Star* he wanted to make the restaurant "the place" for fine dining in Lincoln and brought back much of the original menu from the first Lincoln Underground.

Sadly, the new place didn't take hold. After a six-month trial, Malik changed the restaurant's concept (to Northern Italian) and name (to Spinoza), telling the *Lincoln Star* the Underground "was a little too expensive for Lincoln."

Brittany's Esterhazy Steak

1 small onion
½ green pepper
6 ounces fresh mushrooms
4 ounces butter
½ teaspoon pepper
3 pints au jus
½ cup tomato juice
1 tablespoon sherry
Roux, made of 1 cup flour mixed with ¼ pound butter, melted
4 potatoes
6 carrots
2 onions
18 whole fresh mushrooms
2 pounds sirloin tips
4 tablespoons butter
8 tablespoons sour cream, for garnish

Dice onion and green pepper; slice mushrooms. In melted butter, with pepper added, sauté fresh vegetables until tender. Drain excess butter and add au jus, tomato juice and sherry. Bring to a rapid boil, stirring constantly. Stir in roux gradually until sauce is gravy consistency. Turn heat to low and simmer for one hour, stirring frequently.

Peel and cut potatoes and carrots into bite-size pieces. Boil until tender and drain off water. Peel and cut onions into coarse ½-inch chunks and sauté with mushrooms in 2 tablespoons butter until tender.

Brown sirloin tips in remaining butter.

Combine all ingredients in a large pot with gravy and bring to a low boil. Simmer 15 minutes. Ladle into large, flat bowls and top with 1 tablespoon sour cream before serving. Serve with hot bread. Serves 8.

—Chef's Corner, *Lincoln Star*, November 2, 1983

P.O. Pears

It may take a game of truth or dare for former P.O. Pears owner Bob Jergensen to spill the beans about the lips.

More than eight feet wide, the giant red kisser fronted the kitchen window in the passageway between the front and back rooms at the popular bar and grill on at 322 South 9th Street. Patrons—often using fake names because, well, that was how it was done—ordered and picked up their food at the lips.

Opened in 1980, P.O. Pears was part of Californian Al Ehringer's Grand American Fare chain, which placed bar and grills in college towns. A Western Airlines pilot, Ehringer started with the Oar House Bar & Buffalo Chips Restaurant in Santa Monica in 1964. The Oar House was known for its cheap eats, innovative music and eclectic décor.

Sound familiar?

Jergensen said Ehringer bought a movie warehouse, which supplied many of his restaurants across the country with their unique décor. The memorabilia at P.O. Pears included:

- The ship above the front windows. It was used in in *Tora, Tora, Tora*, *Midway* and *The Sands of Iwo Jima*.
- The sleigh above the front bar. It was from *Dr. Zhivago*, a movie of love and loss in Russia in which everybody dies or at least lives miserably ever after. (Now you know why it was above the bar.)

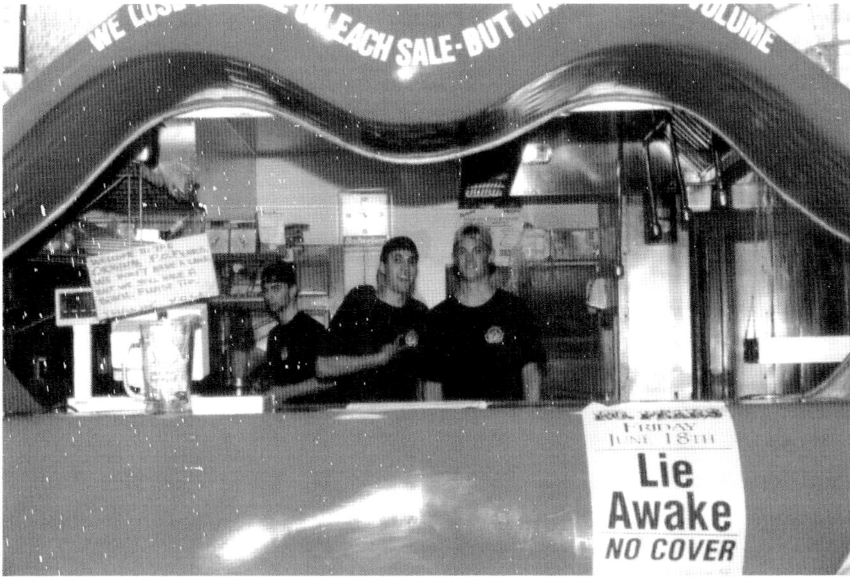

Cooks work behind the lips at P.O. Pears. A flyer advertises Lie Awake, one of the popular cover bands to play the club during the 1990s. *Courtesy of Bob Jergensen.*

- The wheelchair hanging in the back room near the southeast corner of the dance floor. It's purportedly from the movie *Psycho*.

And the lips?

"It's always been said they were from a Rolling Stones concert tour, and to this day I'm going to keep telling people they were," he said. "We'll just leave at that."

Unlike today, students didn't have as many drinking or socializing options, so when Pears opened, it quickly became the place to go.

The tavern was huge—the back bar served as the dance hall, with students gyrating to the sounds of Rick Springfield, the Cars and the Tubes.

The front bar was a great place to mingle, to get away from the noise and flirt with members of the opposite sex.

"I've had more people come back and tell me they met their spouses here," Jergensen told me for a *Journal Star* article I wrote in 2005 about the Pears's twenty-fifth anniversary. Jergensen began working at the bar in 1985, took it over in 1993 and bought the building and land in 1999. He also met his wife there. She was a bartender.

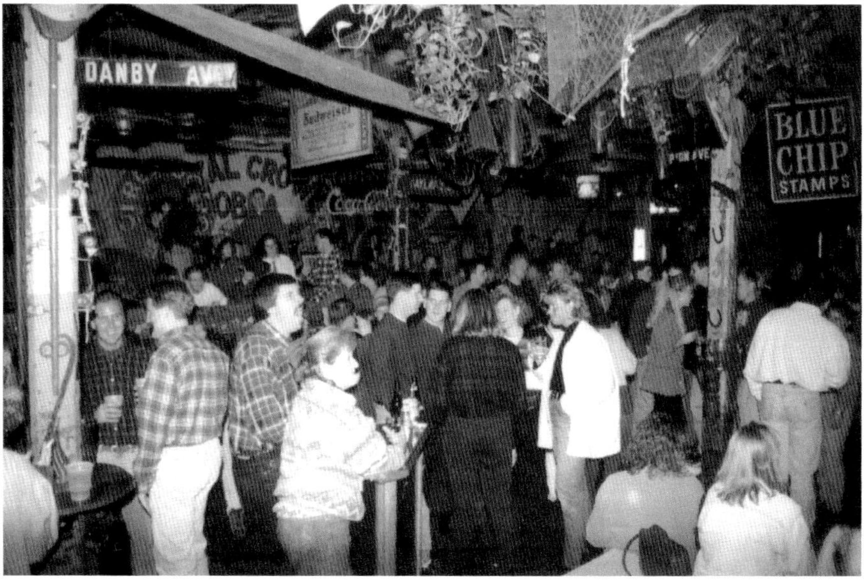

P.O. Pears was a popular destination for college students in the 1980s and '90s—they would pack the back bar, which featured a dance floor. *Courtesy of Bob Jergensen.*

The bar and grill had a party room upstairs. It often was used by fraternities and sororities for social functions.

The décor only added to the appeal. P.O. Pears was hip, a unique museum of sorts.

In the early '90s, downtown Lincoln, specifically O Street between 13th Street and Centennial Mall, filled up with drinking establishments targeting the college market. And Pears, which was off the beaten path, began to lose some of its luster, not to mention its patronage.

In order to survive, the bar began to diversify. In 1993, it added a second sand volleyball court; the first was built in 1985. It began regularly booking the city's top cover bands. Lie Awake used to be a staple. Later, it was groups such as Gigglebox and Groove Puppet.

When hockey came to Lincoln in 1996, P.O. Pears went after the fans, offering them rides in the big red bus to and from Stars games at State Fair Park.

In 1999, Monday Night Big Band found a permanent home in the back room. Two years later, P.O. Pears started booking jazz regularly on Thursday nights, becoming the only place in town to hear jazz consistently.

The biggest draw, though, dated back to opening date: one-third pound of Angus beef between halves of a Rotella bun and lettuce, tomato, red onion and pickles. It was the bar's famous hamburger, the centerpiece of Sundays' and Tuesdays' "Burger Madness." Served with Curly Qs, the burger was a hit with all ages.

Just as popular was the bar's Jiffy Burger, a patty featuring peanut butter, bacon and the fixings.

"I can remember people saying it'll never go, never go, never go, but it ended up being one of the top sellers," Jergensen said. "We had quite a few [burgers], but that's the one people seem to remember."

P.O. Pears served its last Jiffy Burger on March 23, 2008. Jergensen said it was time to close.

"I was getting older, but the kids were staying the same age," he said.

Less than a month after closing, the bar and grill auctioned off its memorabilia, including the lips. They were purchased by a thirty-five-year-old woman from Sterling, who paid $750 for them.

Reuben's

It only made sense a Reuben's would open in Nebraska, since the owners had strong ties to the state.

John McIntosh, who grew up in Omaha, partnered with his Omaha-born brother-in-law Bill McIntyre to create what would become one of the preeminent restaurant groups of its time, the Orange County, California–based Far West Services.

Evolving from the day McIntosh opened a Snack Shop in 1948 in Corona Del Mar, California, Far West's restaurants would come to include Reuben's, Coco's, Reuben E. Lee's, Isadoras, the Plankhouse and many more.

In 1970, Far West became a subsidiary of W.R. Grace & Co. in New York, with McIntosh and McIntyre remaining on board. Two years later, the two men opened a Reuben's in Lincoln at 6100 O Street by the Gateway Mall. At the time, it was one of sixty-five in the country.

For thirteen years, the steakhouse and cocktail lounge became a favorite of Lincoln diners for its prime rib, shrimp scampi and the chicken imperial, an entrée featuring chicken marinated and seasoned with ginger, stir-fried with mushrooms, zucchini, carrots and bean sprouts.

Reuben's was known for its decadent desserts. In 1983, a *Lincoln Star* dining critic called the restaurant "a chocolate lover's paradise" for its Blackout Cake, chocolate mousse pie and German chocolate cake.

The restaurant featured a Spanish motif. Diners sat in leather captain's chairs at cloth-covered tables.

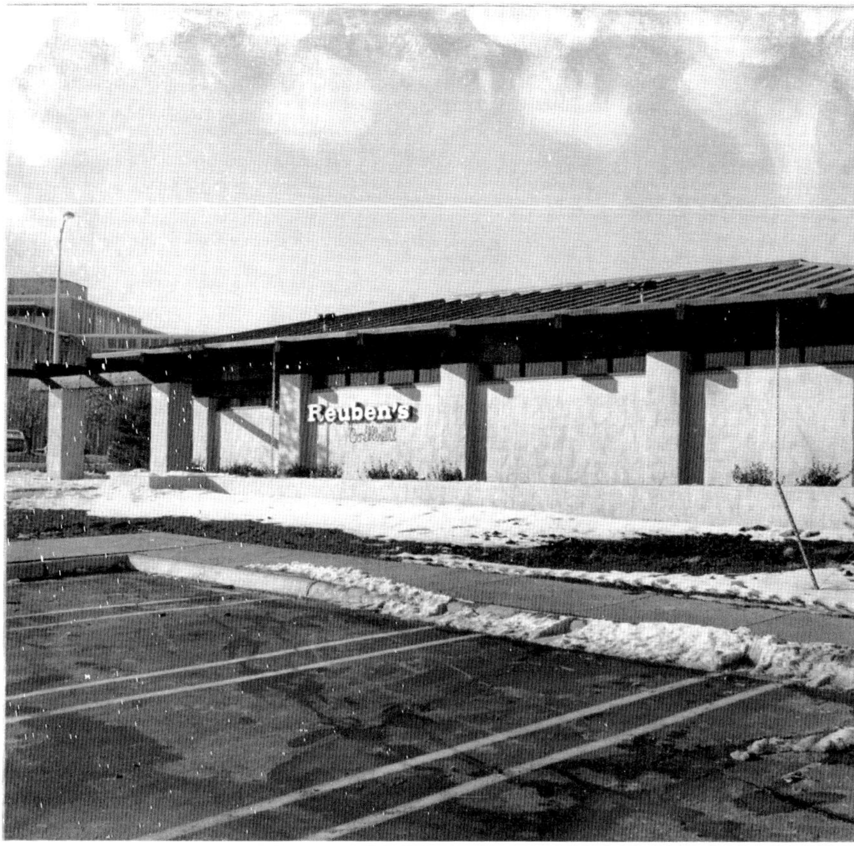

Reuben's opened near Gateway Mall in 1972 and enjoyed thirteen years in Lincoln. *Courtesy of the* Lincoln Journal Star.

Reuben's closed after thirteen years, giving way to a Flakey Jake's hamburger restaurant. But one year later, its sister restaurant Coco's, located at 120 North 66th, began serving a "Reuben's Limited" menu for three hours on Friday and Saturday nights in a dining room set apart from the rest of Coco's.

Reuben's Seafood-Stuffed Mushrooms

2¼ ounces Parmesan cheese
9 ounces scallops, cut into ½-inch cubes and sautéed in butter
5 ounces snow crab

7 ounces cream cheese
9 ounces bay shrimp
Pinch of dry mustard
Salt and white pepper to taste
2 large eggs
24 2-inch mushroom caps
24 ounces prepared hollandaise sauce
Parsley, for garnish

Set aside 1 tablespoon of Parmesan cheese. Mix sautéed scallops, crab, cream cheese, shrimp, remaining Parmesan, seasonings and eggs. Bring 1 cup of water to a boil in a 9-by-13-inch baking pan (use a metal or heat-resistant pan). Place mushrooms in hot water and boil for 2 minutes. Carefully stuff each mushroom with 1½ ounces of seafood mixture. Return to pan, cover and bake at 325 degrees for 10 minutes. Drain and place three mushrooms on each serving plate. Top with homemade or commercial hollandaise sauce. Lightly sprinkle with remaining Parmesan and garnish with parsley. Serves 8.

—Chef Corner, *Lincoln Star*, September 21, 1983

The Rotisserie

Nader Sepahpur is his father's son, having become one of Lincoln's most innovative restaurateurs and bar owners.

Take Amu Manu, for example, Nader's downtown ramen noodle bar. He opened it in 2014, a year after closing his Mexican restaurant, Oso Burrito, simply by posting a sign saying Oso had closed for a "rebirth" and that it would reopen with with a "renewed" spirit.

In downtown's competitive quick-serve market, Nader easily could have gone with sandwiches, burgers or even burritos again.

But he chose ramen noodles, exactly the choice of broke twenty-somethings trying to survive their college years. But Nader's ramen was different; it was his twist on Japanese noodle bowls and Vietnamese pho that nobody else was really was doing in town.

"If it had been somebody else, I would have thought they were kind of crazy," Pete Watters, longtime Zoo Bar co-owner, told the *Lincoln Journal Star* in 2017. "But not Nader. He's just so good at what he does."

His father was much the same way, although the late Bahman "Bob" Sepahpur didn't enjoy the same kind of success.

That's because, as Nader put it, "He was kind of ahead of his time. He was kind of a trendsetter. I guess that's where I get it from."

Bob and his wife and children opened the Rotisserie on the northeast corner of 11th and O Streets in December 1981, coming to Lincoln after fleeing the revolution in Iran. He had operated a restaurant in Tehran, which Nader called a hangout for foreign tourists.

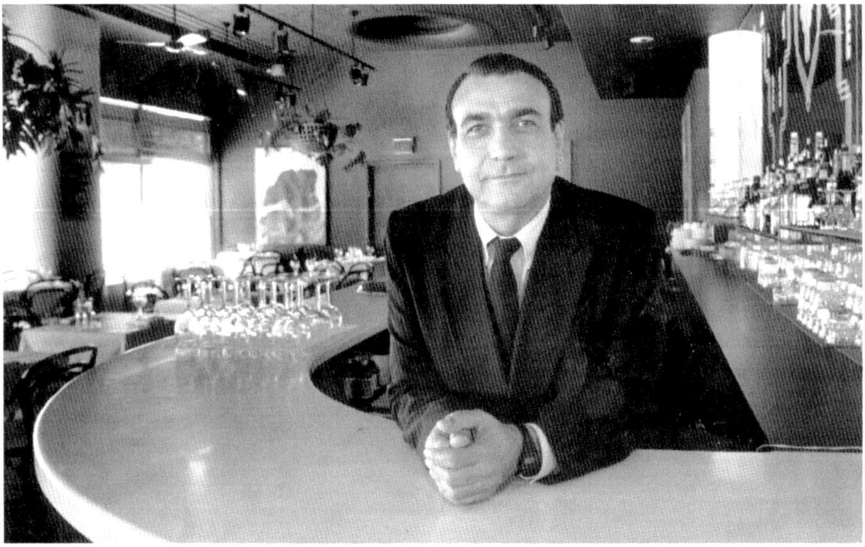

Bob Sepahpur opened the Rotisserie at the corner of 11th and O Streets in 1981. *Courtesy of the* Lincoln Journal Star.

The *Lincoln Journal* called the Rotisserie "luxe," with black bentwood chairs, white tablecloths, linen napkins, classical music, an etched mirror reminiscent of the art deco era backing the bar, touches of brass, plants and nicely attired servers.

Bob topped each table with large, crisp sheets of white paper, which were replaced after each meal. The restaurant encouraged patrons to scribble and draw. "People loved sitting at the table and writing," Nader said.

They also enjoyed seeing the kitchen staff, who, thanks to an open kitchen, were visible from the dining room. Today, open kitchens are common. In 1981, they were a novelty.

"Back then you hid the staff," Nader said. "Back then, it wasn't a reputable occupation. You were cooking or whatever. You used to hide that stuff. But that was my dad's thing, to dress those guys up and have them be up front. He thought it was fun. Instead of chef's hats, they had bicycle hats. I remember that. A couple of the chefs were bikers back then."

The Rotisserie didn't take credit cards—"I'm anti-plastic money," Bob told the *Lincoln Star*—and had a no-tipping policy.

"We charge once," Bob said. "I pay all my overhead and this includes tipping. The tip is part of the employee salary and is not the responsibility of the guest."

The restaurant's name resulted from a custom-made rotisserie at the back of the restaurant for Cornish hen, duck, chicken and more. The restaurant's first menu, according to the *Lincoln Journal*, included a Cornish hen with an orange marinade and kumquats and two half-duck entrees, one with a pomegranate and walnut sauce and the other with a plum sauce and served with Mandarin pancakes, scallions and cucumber wedges.

But Lincoln wasn't ready for rotisserie-style foods—at least not yet.

"He was hoping that was going to be the thing, rotisserie chicken, before Boston Market," Nader said of his father. "Now you see rotisserie chickens in the grocery stores. That was his whole idea, rotisserie chickens."

Of course, Nebraska is beef country, so the restaurant revamped the menu, adding steaks and seafood to complement the rotisserie fare. Nader called the rotisserie one of his father's "wrong ideas." They weren't really wrong, he said, just wrong for the time.

Another of Bob's ideas that didn't initially pan out: the large plate-glass windows, looking out on to 11th and O Streets.

"We were one of the first with windows," Nader said. "No restaurant had windows in this town. All the steak houses were covered up. Tony and Luigi's didn't have any windows. When you walked into a restaurant, there were no windows. The only places that may have had windows would have been the clubs."

Diners could see the people and traffic outside, but the people outside could see in, too.

"People were afraid of windows," Nader said. "People wanted to be in the dark in restaurants. We had to have the half-curtain bistro thing going at one point, so when people sat by the window they didn't feel like people could see them from the outside."

In 1982, the Rotisserie became Lincoln's second restaurant to open a sidewalk cafe. Pontillo's Pizza at 1246 Q Street opened the first in 1981, after the city council liberalized laws restricting outdoor eating establishments.

"It wasn't fancy," Nader said. "We had planters outside and cute little ropes and torches and stuff."

But it didn't work. People weren't comfortable—Nader used the words "freaked out"—sitting outside. The city also didn't allow alcohol outside the restaurant, so customers could order only iced tea and soft drinks.

Today, outdoor seating is prevalent throughout Lincoln's restaurants, with the city again liberalizing its laws and allowing eateries and bars to serve liquor outdoors.

Interestingly, the Rotisserie also faced some indoor seating issues.

"We were stupid enough to be one of the first restaurants that didn't have any booths," Nader said. "People would walk in and look around and say 'Can we have a booth?' I would say 'We have no booths.' They would literally turn around and leave."

Nader began running the family-owned restaurant in 1986. In 1989, the Rotisserie opened a lower-level lounge called the Grotto. It was less formal, and the menu was smaller, less expensive. In 1994, the Sepahpurs moved the concept upstairs and renamed the entire restaurant the Grotto.

The rebranding included a remodel. A high partition divided the bar from the dining room, which used to be open, more communal. Bar-style stools and high tables were added on the bar side of the walls, which reflected the lower level's look.

"The Rotisserie was never intended to be a really formal, uptight fancy place," Grotto manager Herb Thomas told the *Lincoln Journal* in 1994. "However, it did have that reputation to the point where it was almost a stigma. A lot of people felt that they could only go there for special occasions or for lavish meals, and never just to get a good meal at a reasonable price."

Thomas, who passed was away in 2012, had come to the Rotisserie/Grotto in 1989. In 2000, *Ground Zero*, the *Lincoln Journal Star*'s entertainment magazine, declared Thomas the best waiter in Lincoln. He is remembered today as much as the restaurant he called home for more than ten years.

Born in West Germany in 1950, Thomas immigrated to the United States in 1952. He graduated from Lincoln Northeast High School in 1968 and the University of Nebraska–Lincoln in 1972, earning degrees in German and political science.

Thomas didn't set out to become a premier waiter. It just worked out that way. He landed his first job at the Villager during his senior year in college and discovered he enjoyed it. His skills evolved from there. He eventually left Nebraska to live and work in Houston.

He returned to Lincoln in 1977 and worked in a laboratory at the University of Nebraska–Lincoln but soon realized he missed the restaurant business, so he took a position waiting tables at the Lincoln Country Club.

"I like what I'm doing," he told the *Journal Star* in 2000. "I do it because I choose to, not because I have to."

Soon, many of Lincoln's elite restaurants dotted his résumé: University Club, the Lincoln Exchange and Billy's. At the Rotisserie/Grotto, he mixed table service with management. He left Lincoln for San Francisco in 2001.

"People have a notion of what a server or a butler is, from storybooks maybe, even if they've never actually come across one," Nader said. "Herb

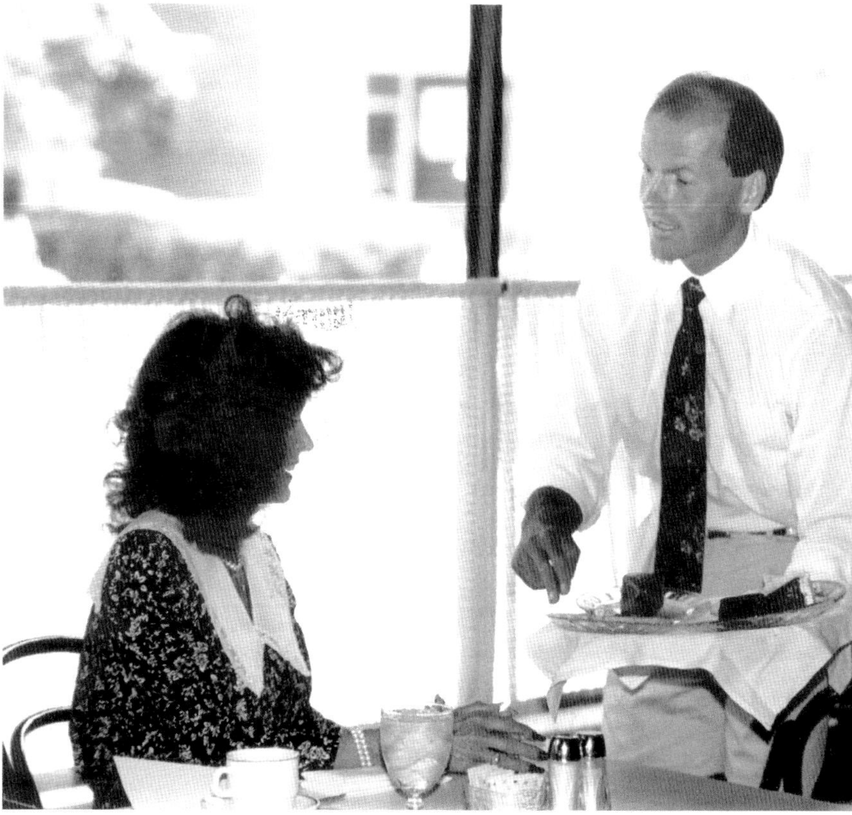

Herb Thomas waits on a diner at the Rotisserie in 1992. Thomas became known as one of Lincoln's top servers. *Courtesy of the* Lincoln Journal Star.

was that character. Maybe you have never met him in your life, but when you met him and he served you, he was this character that you read about in a book or something. He brought integrity to the whole thing of service. He took pride in it. It wasn't like this lowlife job he did."

Nader sold the Grotto in 2002. His father passed away in 2016. The new owner renamed the restaurant Dish, the name it has today. Among Dish's features are outdoor seating and big plate-glass windows. And still, there are no booths.

Skylight Bistro

When the Skylight Bistro opened in March 1982, it offered a menu atypical for Lincoln at the time, with such dishes as cod provencal, lamb marrakech and a fondue bourguignonne: chunks of beef tenderloin cooked by patrons at their tables and dipped into horseradish, barbecue or mustard sauces.

That was the whole point.

Owners Corine Simon and Fyrne Rudorf told the *Lincoln Journal* they intended the restaurant to be "a busy, bustling kind of New York-style cafe for lunch and very relaxed dinner with an international menu and special desserts and appetizers."

The Skylight Bistro introduced me to roast duck, for which I still have a fondness. During my college years, the restaurant at 235 North 11th Street and just a couple of blocks from the University of Nebraska–Lincoln campus was a favorite of mine. My fraternity brothers and I relied on the Skylight Bistro to impress dates on formal occasions. The dining room was small and intimate, with brick walls giving it some character.

When it first opened, the Skylight Bistro served dinner on Friday and Saturday nights only, but it soon it expanded its hours, especially after it closed for two months the following summer, reopening with a new menu, a new manager and some new décor.

In April 1988, Jim Higgins and Doug Nabity bought the bistro from then owner Roger Rhodes and changed the name to simply the Bistro. They wanted to match the overall experience—service, atmosphere, presentation—to the restaurant's food reputation.

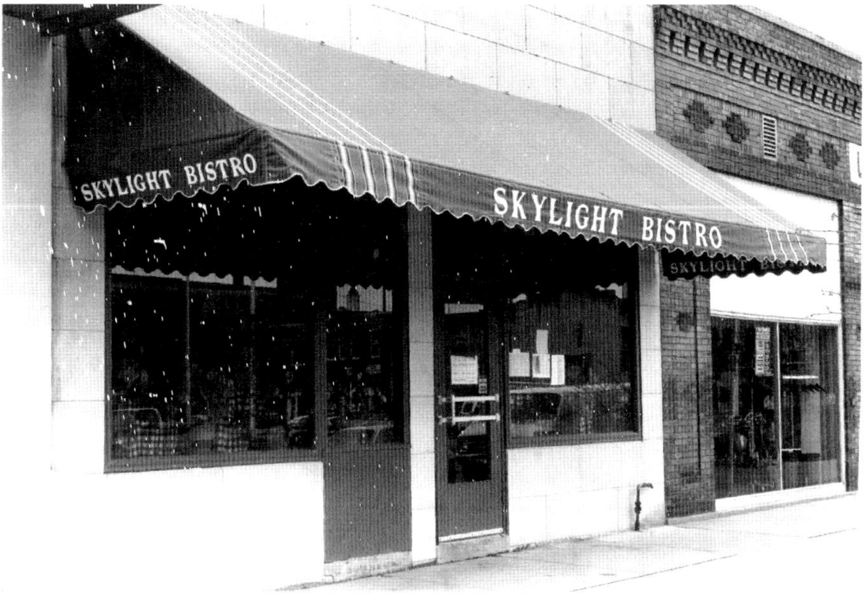

The Skylight Bistro opened in 1982 at 235 North 11th Street and became known for its distinctive dishes. *Courtesy of the* Lincoln Journal Star.

"Getting rich isn't our goal," Nabity told the *Lincoln Star* in May 1988. "Having a neat, successful restaurant that's on the tip of everybody's tongue when they ask where to go out…that's our goal."

Then came the move. Many businesses on the now-infamous Block 35 either closed or located elsewhere when the city decided it wanted to redevelop it. Redevelopment, however, didn't happen until years later.

Meanwhile, the Bistro took up residence about three blocks away at 126 North 14th Street, the former site of Ted and Wally's. It closed its old store on November 18, 1989, and reopened in its new digs six weeks later.

The new place was much bigger, doubling seating to about 150 people in rooms upstairs and downstairs, but the menu maintained its flourish. It included such dishes as chicken dijonnaise, fettuccine bolognese and, of course, the aforementioned duck with a cranberry-orange sauce.

Sadly, the Bistro closed less than two years later. Higgins shut down the restaurant in September 1991, telling the *Lincoln Journal* that lunches, with the built-in business crowd, were good, "but during this recession people have stayed home to eat during the evening. Lied Center events helped, but not as much as we hoped."

Skylight Bistro's Cranberry Pecan Pie

3 eggs
⅔ cup sugar
Salt, a dash
1 cup dark corn syrup
⅓ cup butter, melted
1 cup pecan halves, coarsely chopped
1 cup fresh cranberries, coarsely chopped
1 9-inch unbaked pastry shell

Slightly beat eggs; add sugar and salt, stirring until dissolved. Stir in corn syrup and melted butter. Mix well. Stir in pecans and cranberries. Pour mixture into pie shell and bake at 350 degrees for 50 minutes.

—Chef's Corner, the *Lincoln Star*, December 21, 1983

The Steak House

Earl Vermaas never will forget Saturday, July 2, 1949—the day he opened the Steak House. His partner Harold Winters had advertised the new restaurant, and about one hundred people outside counted down the minutes to the 5:00 p.m. opening.

Vermaas admitted they were not ready.

"The day before the opening, I was still laying tile," the then eighty-five-year-old told me in 1999 for a story I wrote about the restaurant's fiftieth anniversary for the *Lincoln Journal Star*. "We had never cooked one steak, one hamburger or poured one glass of iced tea."

"If anything could go wrong, it did that night. I made more enemies that night than friends."

Winters had asked Vermaas to help him open a restaurant after his old one had burned down, but Vermaas was wary. He ran a successful service station with his brother Roy, but he didn't know anything about the restaurant business.

But he was game to try something new.

"The trouble with partnerships is one guy usually doesn't have any money," Vermaas told me for the story. "[Harold] didn't have any money. Neither did I, but I had a good credit rating."

Vermaas got a $5,000 loan from the bank with no collateral. He and Winters leased a building at 3441 Adams Street, just off of Cornhusker Highway, and purchased equipment from an Omaha restaurant going out of business.

The stone building they rented was built in 1940 of materials recycled from the old Bethany High School. It was supposed to be a beer warehouse, but the owner was unable to secure a license and turned it into a casket factory instead. Later, a nearby machine shop rented it to store fertilizer.

Vermaas and Winters' partnership dissolved quickly. Vermaas said Winters disappeared for fifteen days after opening night. When he returned, Vermaas was waiting with his lawyer. He bought out Winters for $1,500. He had to borrow more money to do it.

"From then on, I got an education in running a restaurant," he told me. "I stuck my neck out and was determined not to lose the money I had in there."

He never borrowed again. He never missed a deadline. And he told himself that if he lasted five years, he was selling it.

Thirty-three years later, he made a call to Larry Snyder.

When Snyder originally offered to buy the Steak House, the peppermint schnapps bottle was empty.

At least that's how he remembered it.

"I tell this story often, but not all of it is totally true," Snyder told me in 1999 as we sat a table with a green-and-white checkered cloth in the cozy dining room of the Steak House. Restaurant manager Joyce Standley, then a thirty-year employee, joined us for the storytelling session.

On a brisk autumn day in western Nebraska, he was duck hunting with his friend Vermaas. They sipped schnapps to fight off the chill and visited as they waited for the ducks. Vermaas said he wanted to sell his popular Lincoln restaurant. Snyder said he would buy it when Vermaas was ready. Months later, Vermaas was ready. He called Snyder at his business. In 1957, Snyder founded Lincoln's Snyder Industries, a manufacturer and supplier of plastic bulk storage, processing and transportation systems.

Snyder remembered the conversation going like this:

"Snyder, it's yours," the voice on the other end said.

"Who is this?" Snyder asked.

"Vermaas, and it's yours," the voice answered.

"What is?" Snyder asked.

"The restaurant," Vermaas responded.

There was a long pause.

"I was a little taken aback at the time," Snyder told me. "And then I'm beginning to remember. It's starting to come back to me. The one thing I remember was the schnapps bottle being empty."

Snyder took over the restaurant in August 1982.

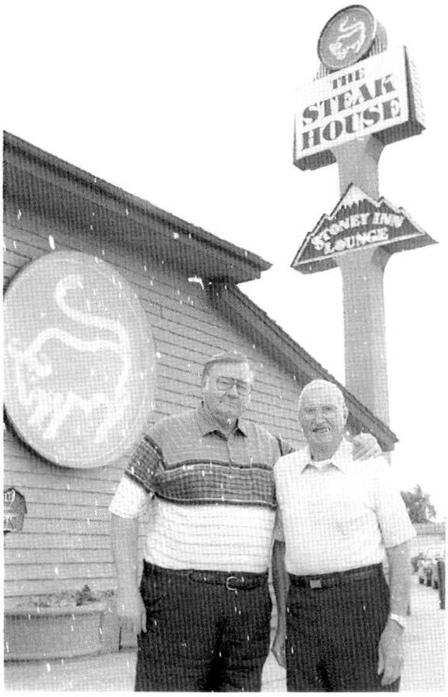

Larry Snyder (*left*) and Earl Vermaas stand outside the Steak House in July 1999, the year the restaurant celebrated its fiftieth anniversary. *Courtesy of the* Lincoln Journal Star.

The first things you noticed upon entering the Steak House were the animals: two moose, a reindeer, a caribou, a buffalo, a golden eagle, a salmon, a northern pike and so on. They were displayed prominently on the walls with descriptive name plates.

Vermaas bagged many of the trophies. Part of the zoo, including the large moose, were on loan from the A.F. Svoboda estate. Former Nebraska Wesleyan basketball coach Jerry Schmutte caught the northern pike and gave it to Snyder.

The restaurant's physical appearance had changed dramatically since Snyder's purchase in 1982. The stone building encompassing the dining room was the same, but the flat roofs were now peaked. The lounge, first installed when liquor laws changed in the mid-'60s, was enlarged in 1985. A fireplace was added about the same time.

In 1990, the forty-five-person party room was built, expanding the restaurant to just more than six thousand square feet. Snyder eventually carpeted the old red and white tile floors.

"I didn't want to put carpet down," Snyder said at the time. "I was afraid people would say, 'What happened to the good old Steak House?'" That didn't happen.

The employees were fiercely loyal. The majority of them were college students who liked the restaurant's flexible hours. Then there are others like Standley, kitchen manager Marlene Fleming and lunch cook Julie Larson, who were as important to restaurant's history as Vermaas and Snyder.

"I've told a lot of people this," Vermaas told me in 1999. "I'm real happy to say I owned the Steak House. It's been a good place since I've been out of here. I've never been ashamed to say I owned the Steak House."

During its heyday, the Steak House became a popular eating place for many celebrities.

Famed country gospel singer Tennessee Ernie Ford ate there. So did Lorne Greene and Dan Blocker, who played Ben and Hoss Cartwright, respectively, on TV's *Bonanza*.

The most regular celeb was comedian George Gobel, who befriended Vermaas and always stopped at the Steak House when performing in Lincoln.

Gobel, known for his crew cut, bow tie and country humor, even tended bar one night, with Vermaas recalling fondly an encounter between Gobel and a patron. The customer ordered a drink and gave five dollars to Gobel, who placed the bill in the cash register. A short time later, the customer asked for his change.

"Anytime 'Lonesome George' fixes you drink, it's worth $5," Vermaas remembered Gobel saying in response.

After owning it nearly twenty-two years, Snyder sold the Steak House in March 2004 to Duane Benkowski. It closed in 2014 and became a used car dealership.

The Steak House's Steak and Mushroom Soup

Joyce Standley shared this recipe with the *Lincoln Star* in 1984, saying she was "experimenting around" in the kitchen one day when she created this cross between a soup and stew. It became a house specialty.

1 pound cubed steak
1 ½ gallons water
½ medium onion, sliced
3 large carrots, sliced
1 stalk celery, diced
½ cup barley
1 cup canned sliced mushrooms
Au jus mix, optional
Kitchen Bouquet, optional

Simmer steak in water until tender. Add vegetables and barley and continue to simmer until all ingredients are cooked and soup thickens. Stir frequently. Add au jus mix and Kitchen Bouquet to own personal taste and to add color. Serves 8 to 10.

—Chef's Corner, *Lincoln Star*, August 29, 1984

Taco Hut / Arturo's

In 1961, there was no Mexican food in Lincoln, fast food or otherwise. So when Arturo and Emilina Longoria opened the Taco Hut at 233 North 11th Street, it proved to be, well, a bit of a hard sell.

"The story my mom tells is that when is that when they first opened up, my grandparents had to adjust the menu so the Anglos would eat the food because they didn't know what Mexican food was," Rene Longoria said. "My grandmother would make pies for the garbage men and postal guys who worked in the mornings, just to get them to come in. Once they were there, she would say 'Hey, this other food is pretty good.' No one knew what Mexican food was."

But they soon learned, falling in love with the Taco Hut's tachas, a food akin to a tostada, with a flat, crisp tortilla loaded with refried beans, ground beef (or chicken) and melted shredded cheddar cheese.

"Our main dish was the tacha," said Daniel Longoria, Rene's brother. "It was something our grandfather coined. It was a combination between a taco and a chalupa. When we first opened up and through the seventies and eighties, those were probably our biggest sellers. It's what we were known for, the tachas."

Tachas are easy to make but not easily replicated at home. Why?

"The secret to that is we made our own shells back then," Rene said. "We made our own tortillas for a long, long time, and our own beans. Everything that was unique about the tacha was because of how we made it."

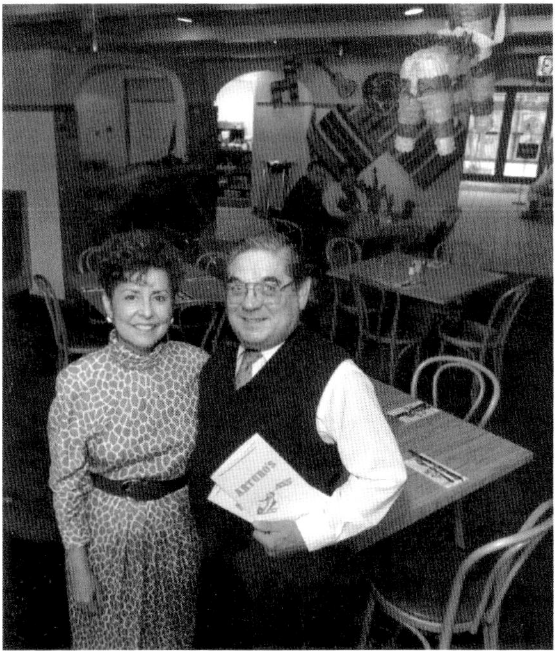

Right: Carmen and Art Longoria Jr. are pictured here in December 1990 inside Arturo's at 801 Q Street, the restaurant's fourth location. *Courtesy of the* Lincoln Journal Star.

Below: The Taco Hut moved to the corner of 11th and Q Streets in 1969 and changed its name to Arturo's ten years later. *Courtesy of the* Lincoln Journal Star.

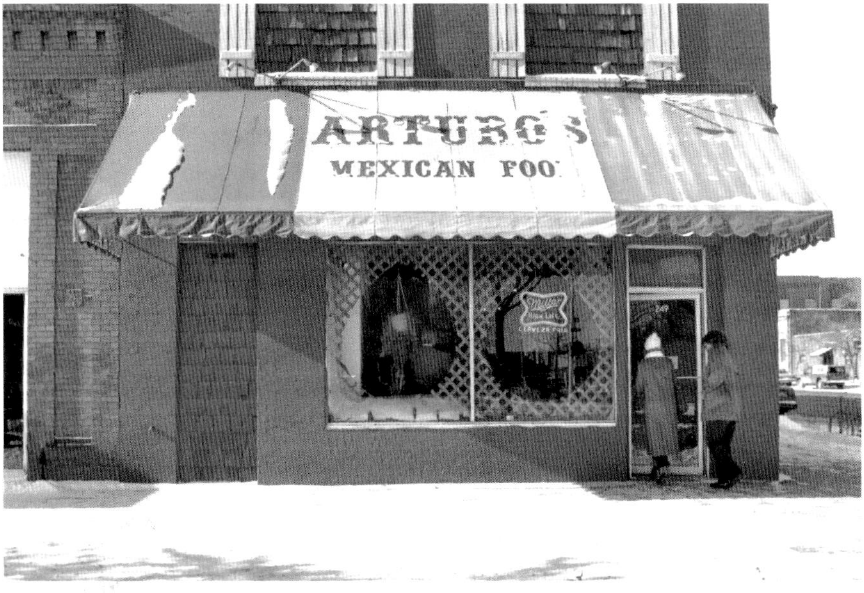

In 1967, Arturo Longoria Jr. and his wife, Carmen, moved their family from California to Lincoln to help his parents run the Taco Hut. Daniel and Rene were eleven and nine years old, respectively, and they remember well their grandparents' restaurant, which sat in the middle of the block.

"It had six booths, three counter stools and a jukebox," Daniel said. "My cousin and I, when somebody would put a dime in the jukebox, we would dance. People would give us a couple of pennies or a nickel. I remember we would be like 'Wow! We made fifty cents today dancing.' They probably paid us to stop." Daniel then laughed at the memory.

In 1969, the Taco Hut moved down the block to the corner of 11th and Q Streets. The move allowed the Mexican restaurant to more than double its seating capacity, from forty to ninety. It needed the extra room. Under the father-son partnership, the Mexican restaurant had become a hit—with all kinds of "hutters."

"It was such an eclectic group of people, from [Nebraska governor] Bob Kerrey to students at the university to the hippies at Dirt Cheap," Rene said. Dirt Cheap was a used record store and and Taco Hut neighbor.

Daniel remembered a Dirt Cheap customer walking into the Taco Hut without shoes. Arturo Jr. told the young man he needed shoes to enter.

"This kid came back with a couple of pieces of cardboard and some string for his shoes," Rene laughed. "My dad let him in. He goes 'all right.' You could have a Woodstock-looking kind of kid and next to him would be Judge [Jeffre] Cheuvront. It was that kind of clientele. Just about anything you would see."

One "hutter" was noted Nebraska artist Keith Jacobshagen, who gave the family an oil painting of a jalapeno pepper that the Longorias hung in the restaurants and later used on the menu cover.

By 1976, Arturo Jr. and Camen's five boys—Artie, Daniel, Rene, Dick and Mike—had become more active in the day-to-day operations, from dishwashing to cooking to management. Rene remembers stacking empty wood Pepsi cases in order to reach the sink to wash dishes.

In 1979, the Taco Hut officially changed its name to Arturo's. In 1987, the city announced it planned to exercise eminent domain to condemn Arturo's, Dirt Cheap and the other Block 35 businesses to make way for a development. Arturo's opened a second location in 1988 at 70th and Van Dorn Streets before closing its downtown store in 1989.

But the development never materialized, and the block bonded by P, Q, 10th and 11th Streets sat as a parking lot for almost a decade before

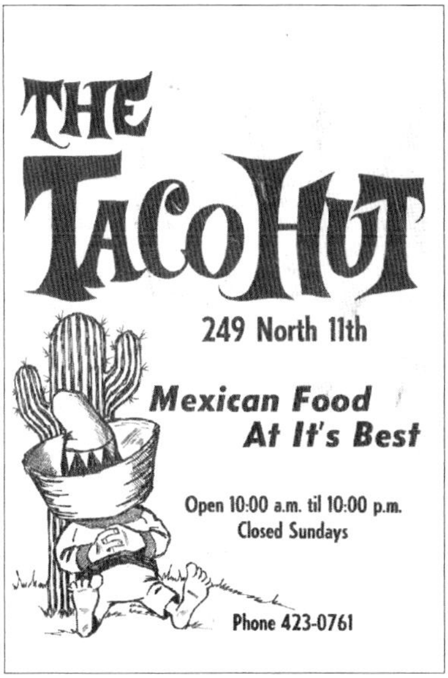

The menu advertises Taco Hut's location, hours and phone number. *Courtesy of the* Lincoln Journal Star.

the Embassy Suites Hotel was built. In 1997—two years after Arturo Jr. passed away—Daniel told the *Lincoln Journal Star* that his father rarely went downtown after the city forced him to move his restaurant because it hurt him "to see a parking lot on the spot where my Dad worked so hard."

In 1998, Arturo's triumphantly returned to downtown, leaving 70th and Van Dorn Streets and reopening on the street level in the historic Port Huron/Huber Manufacturing Building at 801 Q Street in the Haymarket. With its wide-open dining room, it resurrected its feeling of community.

"It's just like the old Hut, on a little bigger scale, of course," Carmen told the *Journal Star* two weeks after opening. "I've had so many different people tell me that."

In June 2007, the family closed the restaurant. Daniel and Rene, who were running it at the time, were ready to move on to something else, plus Rene said "there had been talk of redevelopment" in the Haymarket. "It didn't move as fast as as we would have liked."

Rene hasn't turned his back completely on the business. Once a year, he makes the restaurant's secret recipes for red and green salsas and delivers them to friends and longtime loyal customers.

Today, Mexican food is prevalent throughout Lincoln. But it was Arturo's that led the way. The brothers credit their parents for the restaurant's sustained success.

"My dad was just an incredible people person," Daniel said. "He was really, really funny. He made sure, even up to the end—and my mom was the same way—to stay up front and greet people. They literally would walk around and talk to people and ask 'How's the family?' They would get to know everyone. When we finally closed, we easily were having three generations of families coming in."

Arturo's Tachas

Ground beef (or shredded chicken)
Refried beans
Cheddar cheese
Flat, crisp corn tortilla shells
Jalapeno pepper

Brown ground beef in skillet. Layer refried beans, ground beef and cheddar cheese atop a flat, crisp corn tortilla shell. Place under broiler until cheese is melted. Top with slices of jalapeno peppers.

—Courtesy of Rene and Daniel Longoria, Arturo's

Tony and Luigi's

Put cousins Mike Alesio and Tony "Sonny" Messineo, two men of Sicilian heritage in a room, ask them about food, then sit back and listen.

Listen to a story about the sirloin steak served at Tony and Luigi's, the one marinated in Italian dressing, sealed with bread crumbs and cooked under a broiler.

> *Messineo: We would serve it with a nice little side of pasta, a nice garlic roll. Oh, God. It was very famous, very famous. It was very tender.*
> *Alesio: I could eat that now.*
> *Messineo.: Phenomenal food. Phenomenal food. I don't even remember ever getting a complaint. It was that good. And his* [Mike's] *father, he would come out in that silk suit. He would go out there and meet the people.*
> *Alesio: Dad had tailor-made clothes.*
> *Messineo: Hair slicked back. He was the entrepreneur's restaurateur. Everything you think about an Italian steakhouse, he embodied. He really did. Has was that good.*
> *Alesio: He really was.*

Today, Alesio and Messineo run Valentino's, the historic pizza chain that started in Lincoln and now has locations throughout Nebraska, but both cut their teeth in food service learning at the feet of Mike's father and Tony's uncle. That would be Tony Alesio, co-founder of Tony and Luigi's, which many consider the best Lincoln restaurant ever.

After returning from World War II, Tony Alesio formed a partnership with Louis Demma to buy the Blue Willow, a "spike joint" at 5140 O Street in 1945 for $2,000. They grossed $6.50 on their first day and $18,000 the first year, according to newspaper reports.

"It was a little shack out there, way out on O Street," Mike Alesio said. "It was really in the sticks at that time, pretty tough clientele out there. Let's just say there was a lot of uncultured drinking at that time. It was tough at closing time because everybody was schnockered and didn't want to go home. They had dust-ups there that dad was involved in and my uncle Lou."

Tony Alesio, who admitted to not being able to boil water when he and Demma opened the restaurant, had a plan—a recipe, you could say, for success:

> *Mike Alesio: They started with and focused on their food and were able to add Italian dishes, not only pasta but chicken cacciatore, which you can't get anymore.*
> *Messineo: Nobody.*
> *Mike Alesio: I mean it would come in a clear, glass bowl with a sauce.*
> *Mike Alesio and Messineo* [at the same time]*: Oh my, God!*
> *Mike Alesio: It was so good. So they built up a reputation there.*

Tony Alesio and Demma remodeled in 1951, the first of two remodels—the second came in 1957—before a major rebuild in 1966. Alesio bought out Demma in 1952 and became the face of Tony and Luigi's until he retired in 1978, when Mike Alesio and Tony and Ron Messineo took it over.

"He was probably the best restaurateur there ever was, hands down," Messineo said.

> *He was extremely creative. He could always see farther down, not just the immediate. That's shown on his expansions. He was always ahead of that.*
>
> *But secondly, he was a stickler, demanding in the quality of the food. Never would sacrifice that. The service....I would remember the training sessions he would always have with the servers—they were waitresses then—and he would get them all together at four o'clock and say "This is what I want to get done." And cleaning was second to none. He had a special guy come in every Saturday to clean fixtures. Those three things were the most important to him: the food quality, the service and the cleanliness. He was exacting on that.*

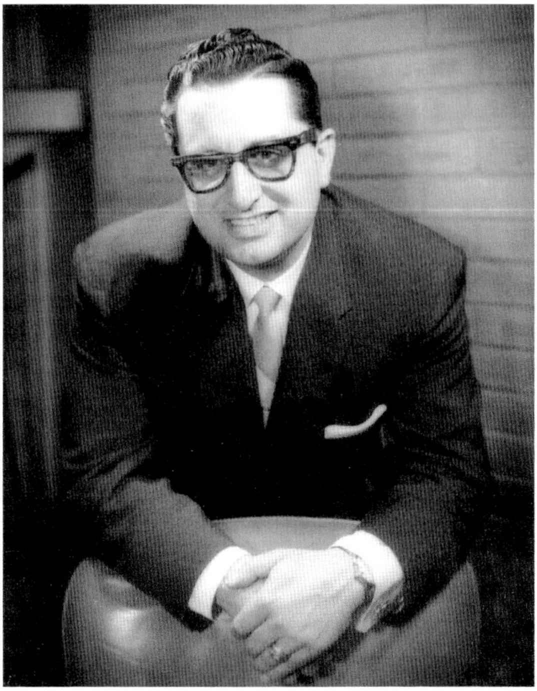

Right: Tony Alesio co-founded Tony and Luigi's with Louis Demma in 1945 and bought out Demma in 1952. *Courtesy of Mike Alesio.*

Below: Tony Alesio samples a sauce in Tony and Luigi's kitchen. *Courtesy of the* Lincoln Journal Star.

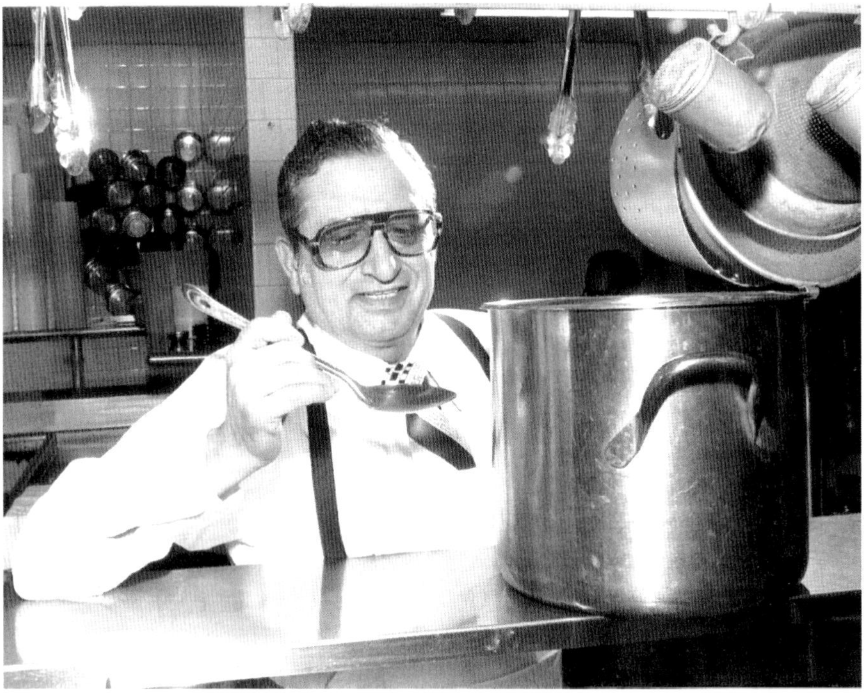

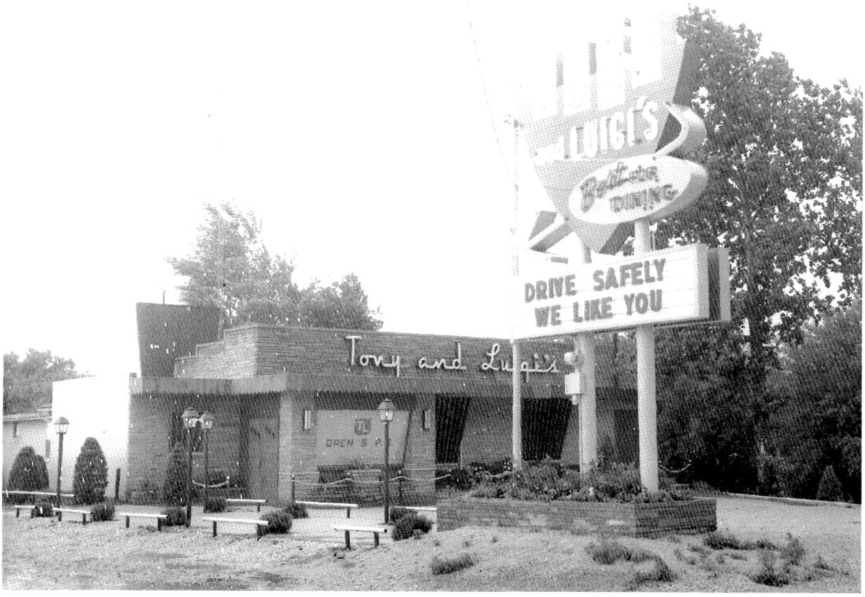

Tony and Luigi's as seen in the 1950s, with a sign advertising the "best for dining." *Courtesy of Mike Alesio.*

During those early years, patrons brought bottles of liquor in paper sacks and ordered bowls of ice and set-ups. In 1963, Tony and Luigi's became one of the first restaurants to apply for a bottle club license under a new state law, but it didn't come without controversy. According to newspaper accounts, city officials felt Tony and Luigi's couldn't operate as a restaurant and bottle club at the same time—it either had to be one or the other. Bottle clubs were allowed to dispense liquor by the drink to members and their guests. The city attorney later determined dual operation was permissible. In December 1966, Lincoln allowed liquor-by-the-drink sales for the first time since 1917.

In 1966, Tony and Luigi's increased its seating from 200 to 325 with a major renovation. Dining areas bore names such as Sicilian, Venetian, Gondola (there was a boat on the wall), Roma and Melody (where the music happened). For many years, Lincoln radio personality Fleda Ziegenbein played the organ, and on New Year's Eve, Tony Alesio led a singalong.

On weekends, especially when the Nebraska football team played at home, each of those areas would be full. On football Saturdays, a line of people waiting to eat snaked around the back of the restaurant. The cousins estimated they fed more than 1,400 on those nights.

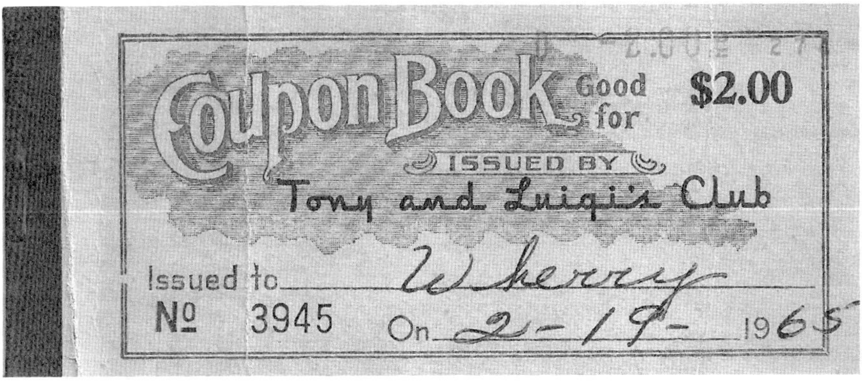

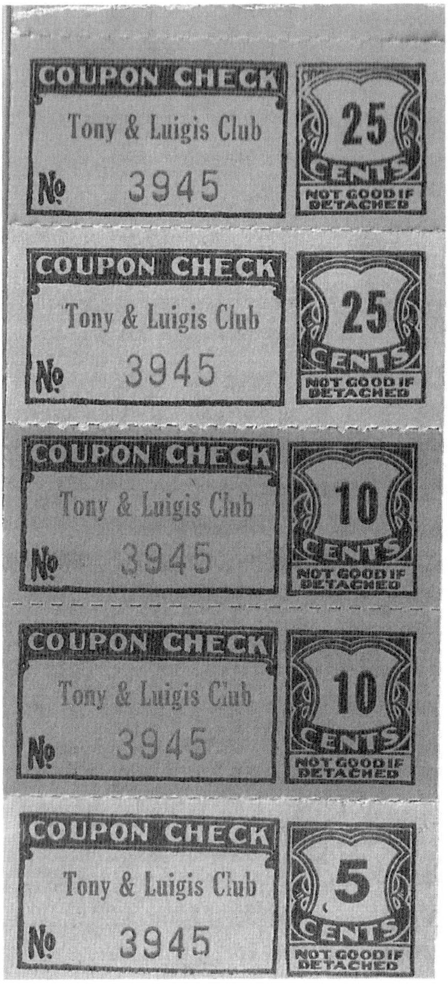

Above: In 1965, patrons used coupons to purchase liquor at Tony and Luigi's. *Courtesy of Anthony Messineo.*

Left: Coupons to purchase alcohol advertise Tony and Luigi's as a Lincoln supper club. *Courtesy of Anthony Messineo.*

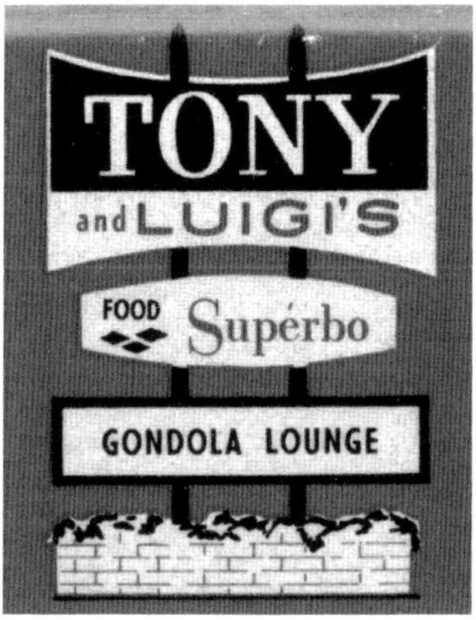

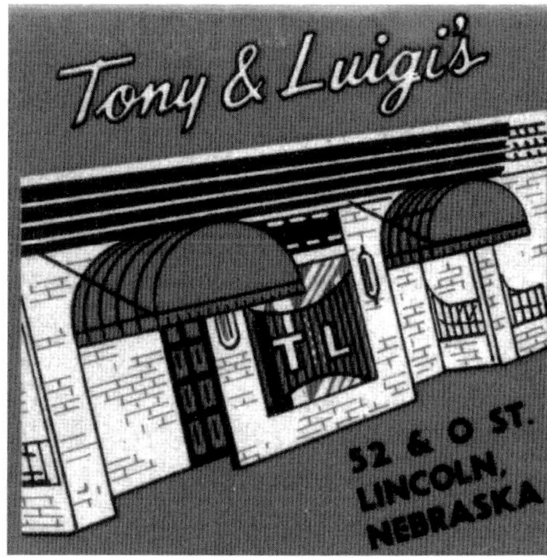

Left: The back of a matchbook advertises the Gondola Lounge, one of the Tony and Luigi's many dining areas. *Right*: The front of a matchbook advertises Tony and Luigi's with a drawing of the building at 52nd and O Streets. *Courtesy of Anthony Messineo.*

Messineo: That's a lot of people. I mean we moved them. And remember these were steaks. I took time to prepare these.
Mike Alesio: Big-time steaks, big time. You don't see that kind of steak anymore.
Messineo: No, you don't see that kind anymore. God, no....You couldn't afford to put that on a plate."
Mike Alesio: You couldn't.
Messineo: What were they, twenty-ounce T-bones?
Mike Alesio: Yeah.
Tony: Oh, God...people use to love those things.

They also loved Tony's cheese-and-onion dip, minestrone soup and the heaping portions of pasta smothered in house-made sauces.

"I think it's fair to say, a lot of those sauces—the cacciatore sauce, the marinara sauce, the spaghetti sauce—were all recipes handed down over the generations," Messineo said. And Tony and Louis, without changing the recipe, developed a commercial use for them, commercial-sized batches.

Tony Alesio even created and trademarked a steak. "It was called the 'Nebrascut,'" Messineo said. "It was a strip sirloin, a New York strip. He would cut a notch out of it, and it would look like the state of Nebraska. It was very popular."

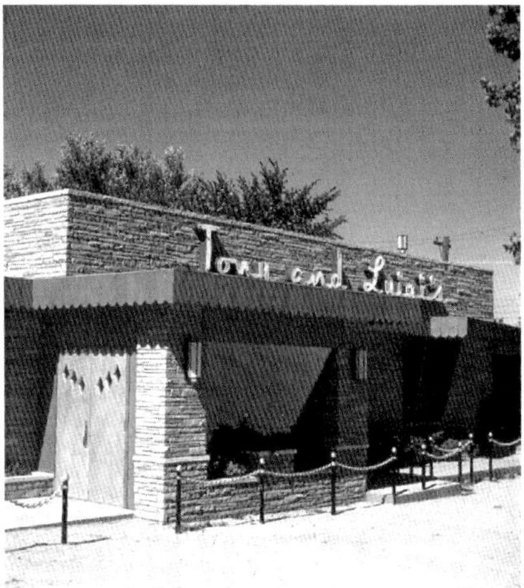

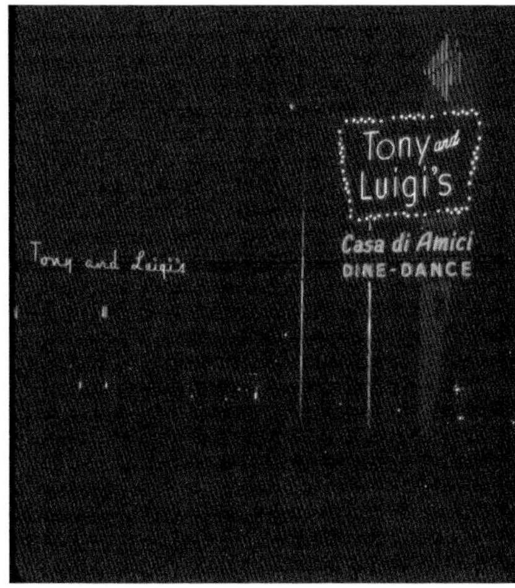

Left: At Tony and Luigi's zenith (1960–80), a line of people would snake out the front door of Tony & Luigi's and around to the back of the restaurant on weekends. *Right*: Neon signs beckon at passersby on O Street to dine at Tony and Luigi's. *Courtesy of Mike Alesio.*

With its reputation firmly in place, Tony and Luigi's began to attract the famous. Celebrities such as Bob Hope, Henry Mancini, Roy Rogers and Dale Evans, Jim Nabors and Captain Kangaroo dined there.

Mike Alesio remembered heading to the restaurant one night to pick up his father only to learn from one of the employees that Tony Alesio wasn't ready yet. He was entertaining Robert Taylor in the Venetian.

"You mean Robert Taylor at KOLN-TV?" Mike Alesio asked. "He said 'No, I mean *Robert Taylor*.' I go in there and sure enough Dad's sitting in there with Robert Taylor and Robert's friend, Russ [Gibson], and they're just eating pizza and pasta and talking. So I just sat down with Robert Taylor, and I remember people were coming up and gawking and going 'That *is* Robert Taylor.'"

In 1983, five years after Tony Alesio's retirement, Tony and Luigi's underwent a face-lift. Four years later came a $250,000 rejuvenation with the intent of giving it a more casual feel in an attempt to compete with the popularity of the city's Mexican restaurants.

"We wanted to make Tony's more fun, more relaxed and have more reasonable prices, while keeping our old favorites," Messineo told the *Lincoln Star*. "I think the Italian restaurant concept will surpass Mexican in drama."

At least, the giant tomato out front provided some drama. The renovation included a 4½-foot-tall, 559-pound ceramic tomato on a pedestal by the entrance. According to the *Lincoln Star*, longtime Tony's patrons wrote letters

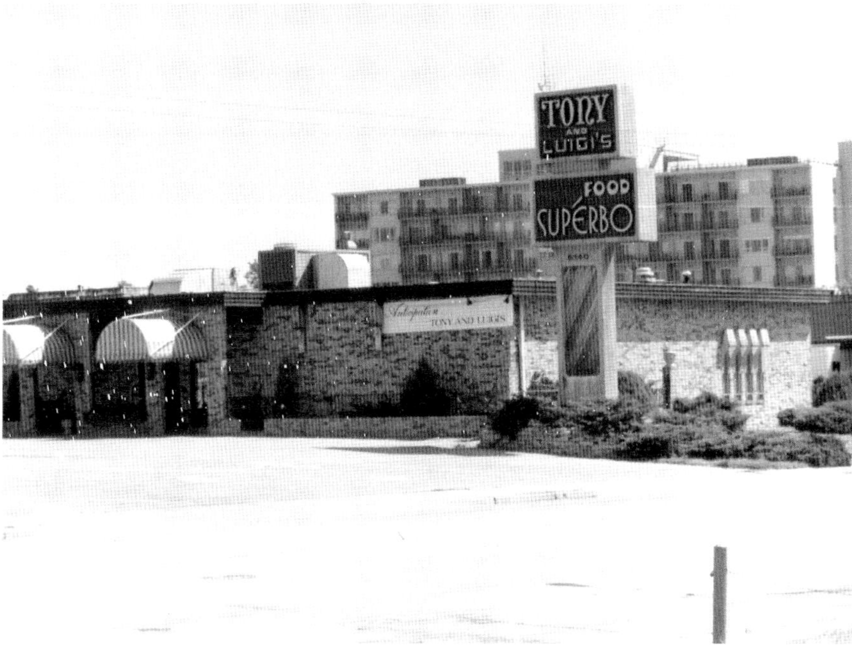

Tony and Luigi's as seen in the 1970s or '80s with a sign advertising "Food Supérbo." *Courtesy of Mike Alesio.*

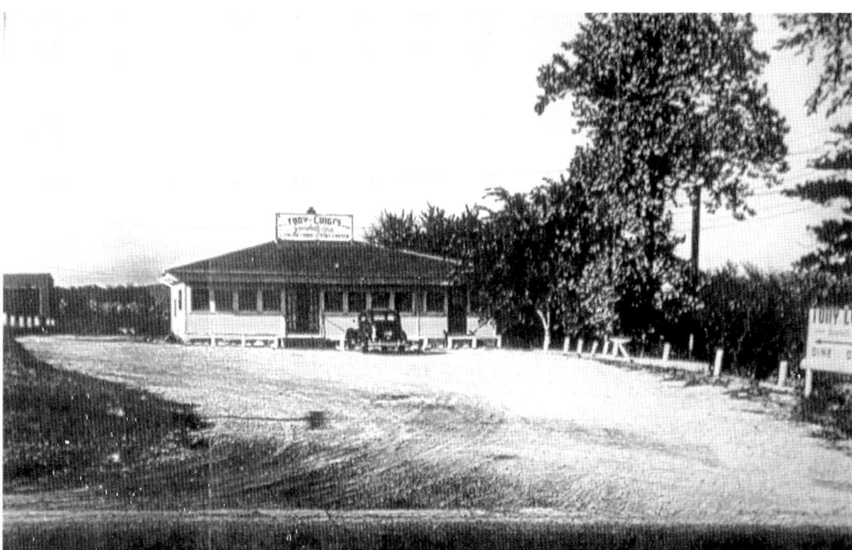

Tony Alesio and and Louis Demma took over a chicken restaurant in 1945 at 5140 O Street and turned it into the Italian eatery, Tony and Luigi's. *Courtesy of Jim McKee.*

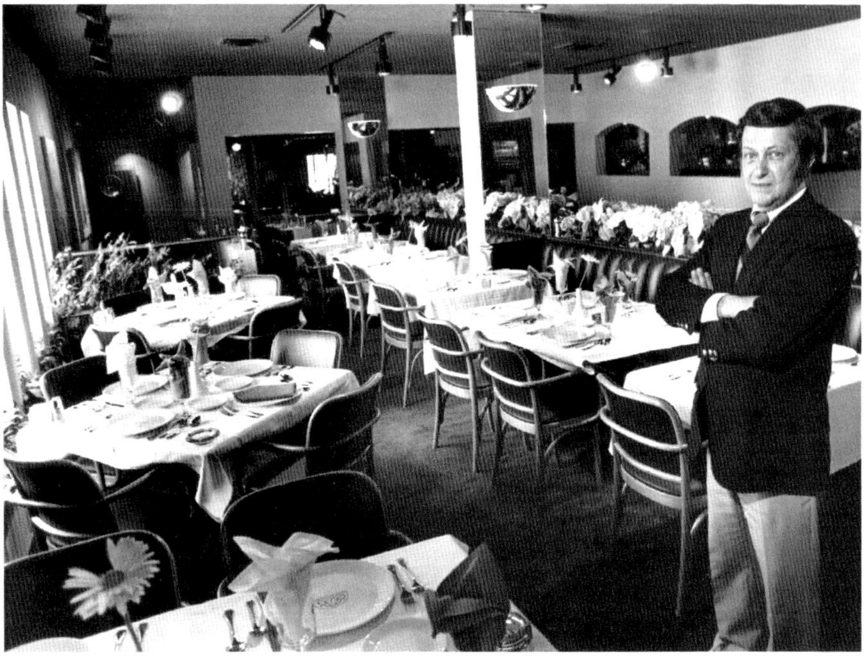

Tony and Luigi's manager Dave Harrison awaits diners at a renovated Tony and Luigi's in May 1983. *Courtesy of Lincoln Journal Star.*

protesting the "eyesore" in front of their favorite restaurant. During the winter of 1988, the restaurant gave it to a customer who came closest to guessing its weight.

Wanting to focus more on Valentino's, Mike Alesio and the Messineos sold Tony and Luigi's in 1989 to former Valentino's executive Joe Buda, who ran it until May 1993. Today, a Barnes and Noble sits on the site. Tony Alesio died in December 8, 2004, at age eighty-six.

"It had a reputation, quite frankly," Messineo said.

> *It became an institution in this city. Everybody, whether it was family gatherings, anniversaries or someone proposing, it was all tied around Tony and Luigi's. I still hear that now.*
>
> *We've had requests to reopen Tony and Luigi's, but it takes that real special individual like Tony Alesio. It's not only food, service and cleanliness. It's that culture that I don't think we can replicate anymore. It was different, just different. He was the persona there.*

Tony and Luigi's Chicken Parmigiana

8 ounces mozzarella cheese
2 ounces cheddar cheese
1 ounce Parmesan cheese
4 7-ounce boneless breasts of chicken, skinned
Seasoned flour (with salt and pepper)
Butter
¾ quart marinara (spaghetti) sauce

Shred and mix the cheeses. Set aside. With a meat hammer, flatten the chicken to a thickness of ½ inch. Coat with seasoned flour and sauté in butter over medium heat until completely cooked. Coat a baking pan with a thin layer of marinara. Place chicken in pan and cover with remaining marinara, paying attention to the edges. Sprinkle cheese mix over chicken and bake at 350 degrees until cheese browns. Serve with pasta. Serves 4.

—Chef's Corner, the *Lincoln Star*, June 27, 1984

CAFÉS, DINERS AND DRIVE-INS

Acme Chili Parlor

Though its recipe was a secret, there was no dish better known to Lincoln diners in the early twentieth century than the "genuine Mexican chili" at the legendary Acme Chili Parlor.

In 1980, Chris Christopulos told the *Sunday Journal Star* that his father, A.C. Christopulos, who opened the café in 1909 at 14th and O Streets, had obtained the chili recipe from a man whose wife was sick and owed A.C. money.

"I don't know when I can pay you," the man told A.C., "but here's a recipe for real Mexican chili. You can't give it to anyone else. It's just for you."

As the *Journal Star* noted, the recipe was A.C's., but the chili was for everyone. It was so hot and greasy that the kitchen served a side of vinegar to temper the grease and a pitcher of ice water to cool the taste buds.

Among those who enjoyed a bowl of the greatest chili around were aviator Charles Lindbergh, actors Jimmy Stewart and Clark Gable and Governor Charles Bryan, brother of William Jennings Bryan.

Believed to be the first Greek immigrant to settle in Lincoln, A.C. came to the United States in 1899 from Tricorsa, Greece, and to Lincoln in 1902. Before opening the chili parlor, he ran shoeshine parlors in Lincoln, York and Hastings, Nebraska; Sioux City, Iowa; Minneapolis, Minnesota; and St. Joseph, Missouri.

A.C. owned the one-story building, with fifty feet of O Street frontage, extending north to the alley on 14th Street. The family operated the chili

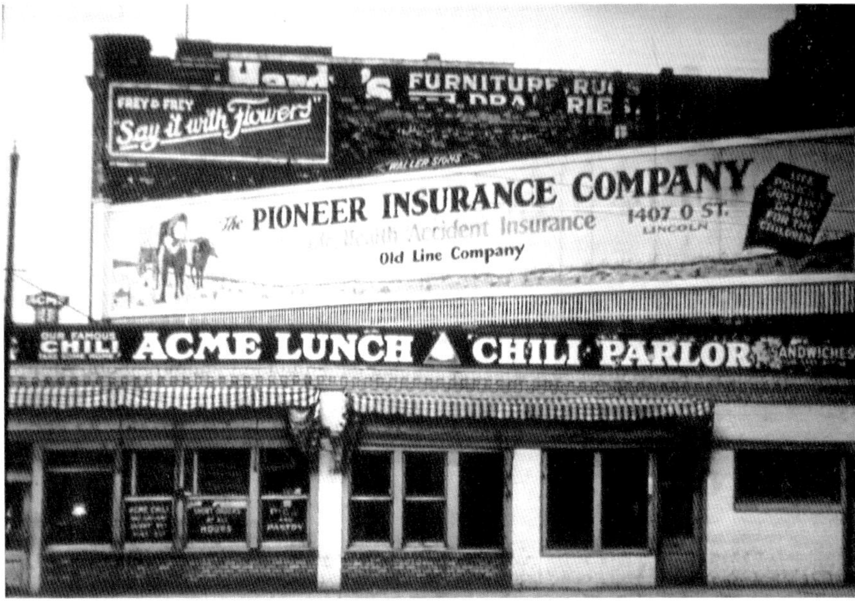

Acme Chili Parlor at 14th and O Streets served enough chili during its fifty-four years "to float the State Capitol," according to the *Lincoln Star*. *Courtesy of Jim McKee.*

parlor there from 1909 to 1963, when it sold the business and recipe to longtime Lincoln chef Glenn G. Morrison.

A.C. was known as much for his work for the YMCA as he was for his famous chili. When he died in March 1967 at the age of eighty-five, he had been a YMCA member for sixty-five years, active in recruiting new members. He was one of the early founders of the Greek Orthodox Church in Lincoln, a longtime member of the chamber of commerce and ran "chop houses" at 1340 O Street and 118 South 11th Street.

The chili parlor also served hamburgers, steaks and stew, but it became primarily successful because of the chili, with the recipe remaining carefully guarded during the restaurant's fifty-four-year run. Even the cooks didn't know exactly how to make it because family members mixed the spices, son Chris told the *Sunday Journal Star*.

Bishop Buffet

Chef Benjamin Franklin Bishop started a restaurant concept that emphasized simple.

"Eliminate the printed menu," he said. "Show people a wide variety of attractive foods and let them put together their own meals. Then provide the benefit of a full-service restaurant."

In 1920, his concept first became a cafeteria in Waterloo, Iowa, and eventually evolved into a restaurant chain.

Bishop Cafeteria, also known as just Bishop's, opened in Lincoln in 1956 at 1325 P Street. The restaurant moved to a ten-thousand-square-foot building at the Gateway Shopping Center in 1972 and was renamed Bishop Buffet. The new restaurant featured four dining rooms with seating for 258. It could serve 50 buffet-line customers every 15 minutes.

The restaurant developed a loyal following, particularly among diners ages fifty-five and older and large families. In 1985, the *Mobil Travel Guide* rated Lincoln's Bishop Buffet as one of the best cafeterias in the country.

During its heyday, Bishop's had ten meats, ten vegetables, twelve salads and twelve pies from which to choose. It was known for its roast beef, fried and baked chicken, baked fish and, of course, its royal chocolate ambrosia pie, which customers, after turning on the signature table lamp to signal a server, often would order a second slice of.

In 1988, it began offering all-you-can eat dining to compete with others offering the concept.

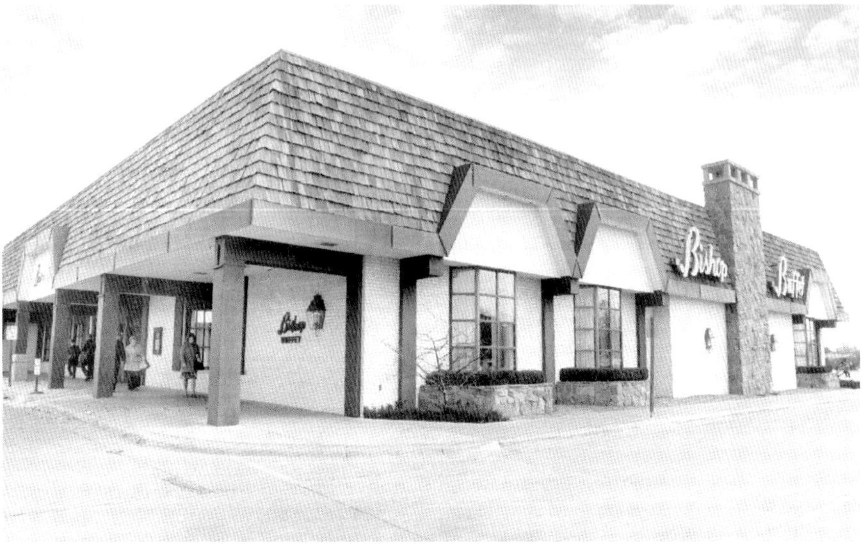

Bishop Buffet opened in Lincoln in 1956 and moved to its location at the Gateway Mall in 1972. It closed in November 1996. *Courtesy of the* Lincoln Journal Star.

"It's kept our previous clients happy and brought a new trend of customers into the cafeteria," Lincoln manager Bill Klinkenberg told the *Lincoln Star* in September 1988. "Some people just don't like to be told no. They like to go back for more. I think it's [the all-you-can-eat format] the wave of the future," he said.

At the time, it surely was, with several buffets opening in Lincoln over the next few years. As diners became more health conscious, the trend began to fade. In 2018, only a handful of buffets still exist.

After forty years in the capital city, Bishop's closed in Lincoln in November 1996. Increased competition from other restaurants led to its demise.

"All you have to do is drive down the streets of Lincoln and see what it going on in the food service industry," a Bishop's executive told the *Lincoln Journal Star*. "Competition has just exploded."

Greenwich Cafe

In his book *Inside Lincoln*, famed Nebraska folklorist Roger Welsch had this to say about the Greenwich Cafe: "The Greenwich doesn't LOOK like England, but it sure does TASTE like England."

The credit for that goes to University of Nebraska–Lincoln botany professor John B. "Doc" Davidson, who in the early 1970s introduced English-style fish and chips to the longtime café at 1917 O Street.

As the story goes, Doc asked Millie Weiler, who ran the popular downtown café with her husband, Francis Weiler Jr., if he could rent the café to feed sixty of his colleagues his very own perfected-over-time battered Icelandic cod.

"I have probably put a few kegs of beer down here with Millie," Davidson told the *Sunday Journal and Star* in 1976.

Millie responded with a question of her own: "Are you a cook?"

His meal, according to the newspaper, was met with such success that Davidson continued frying fish on Friday nights, which later evolved into Friday and Saturday nights. When Doc passed away in 1984, his wife, Jane, continued to fry fish for Greenwich customers.

Growing up in Vancouver, British Columbia, Doc developed a love for seafood. When he and Jane traveled from Lincoln with their children, they often sought ought good fish in local eateries. Those trips resulted in sampling many batters, leading him to develop his own secret recipe.

Doc preferred Icelandic cod because it has fewer bones. He dipped his bite-size pieces into his batter, fried them for a very short time in a cool fryer

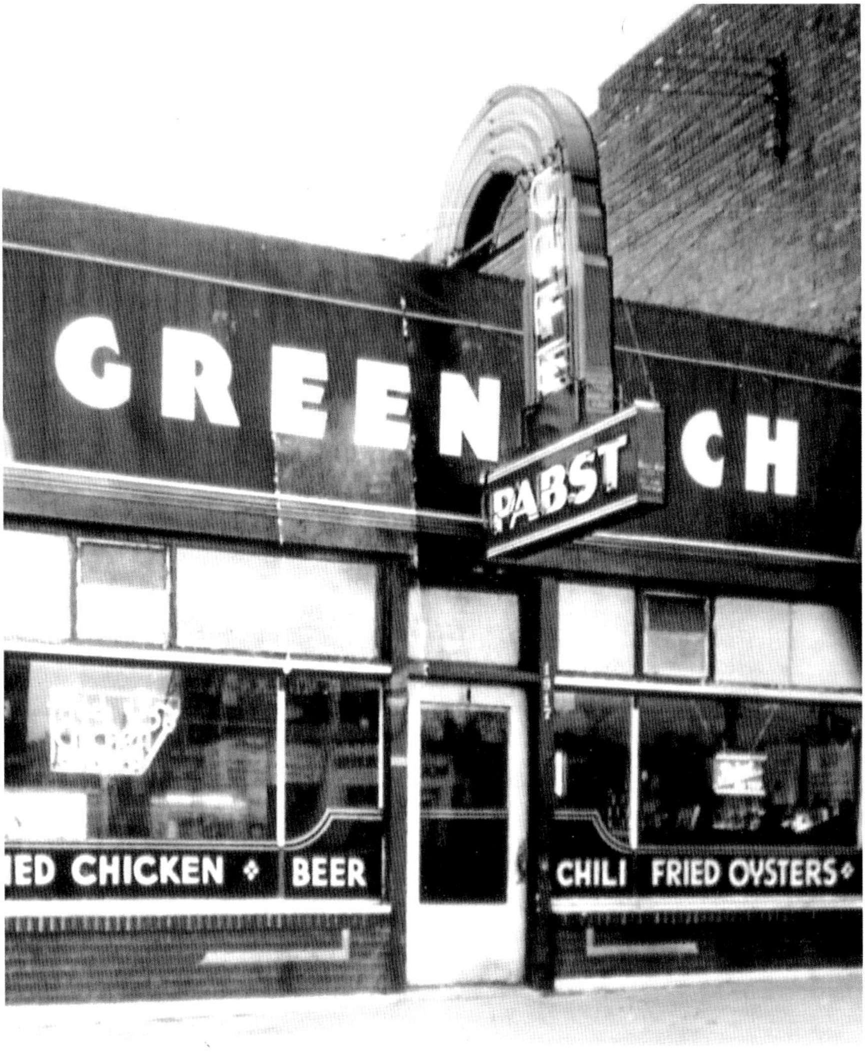

Named for Greenwich Village in New York, the Greenwich Cafe operated at 1917 O Street from 1934 to 1985. *Courtesy of Jim McKee.*

to seal the crust and keep juices in and then transferred them to a hot fryer, where the cooking was completed.

"If done properly in the deep fryer, the fish will be steamed inside the batter—nice, juicy and tender," he told the *Sunday Journal and Star*.

Today, many Lincoln restaurants serve fish and chips, and several Lincoln churches hold fish frys during Lent, but none has come close in reputation to the Greenwich Cafe. Newspapers often wrote of the café's penchant for fish, with two articles referencing the sign that hung behind the bar: "Fish and Chips. Great cod! What food these morsels be."

Francis Weiler Sr. opened the Greenwich Cafe on July 4, 1934, naming it after Greenwich Village in New York City. Even then, the café was known for fish. The following year, the café advertised twenty-to-thirty-cent fish dinners and fifteen-cent oyster stew in the newspaper. Beer and ale were on tap; Prohibition had ended, after all.

Millie started working there in 1939. Her plan was to stay a week and earn some quick cash. She stayed forty-six years. After seven years at the café, she married the owner's son, Francis "Francie" Weiler Jr., whom she had known when she started working there. The two of them continued to operate the café after Francis Sr. died in 1969.

The restaurant, with its rough-around-edges look—a *Lincoln Star* reviewer said the café couldn't "be noted for a swank decor, but it's definitely distinguished"—became a Lincoln favorite, developing a loyal clientele.

"God I tell you, they used to line up in front of here all day," Millie told the *Lincoln Journal* in 1985. "Ask anybody. We wouldn't even let people drink beer in the booths (because the food customers were waiting)."

Millie closed the Greenwich Cafe on October 19, 1985, after fifty-plus years. Her last night was a surprise party for her planned by longtime customers and friends. "Oh God, you wouldn't believe the people who come in here just to see me," she told the *Journal Star*.

She closed because her lease had expired. Keeping it open would have required her to renegotiate a new lease or buy the building, and, at age seventy-two, she said she was too old for that. Plus, Francie needed her. He had lost his sight and a leg to diabetes. He passed away just over two months later.

Millie died in 2003. Her obituary noted she owned the Greenwich Cafe, enjoyed gambling and her friends and was a big Nebraska football fan.

Ken Eddy's Drive-In/Eddy's Restaurant

In 1988, four years after Lu Gold sold her husband's legendary gathering place, hundreds of people came together at the Villager Motor Inn to pay tribute to Eddy's Restaurant.

Gold, to say the least, was moved. It was she, after all, who had told the *Lincoln Journal* in 1980 that she would have loved to rename Eddy's "The Meeting Place."

"We got a variance of people," she told the *Sunday Journal Star* prior to the reunion. "Insurance workers, people from nearby car lots, senators and lobbyists and professors who knew their students wouldn't be here."

From its beginnings, Eddy's, at 4750 O Street, and Ken Eddy's before that, had drawn people—so much so, that the restaurant is remembered as a Lincoln icon.

It all started in September 1948, when Eddie Gold purchased a 178-by-200-foot lot at the northwest corner of 48th and O Streets from University of Nebraska journalism professor Robert P. Crawford. Gold said at the time he had "no plans of any kind" for the property.

Here's guessing that he did. In August 1951, he secured a permit to build a new drive-in café—a building twenty-two by fifty-six feet with a height of thirteen feet. He estimated the cost for the one-story structure at $22,000.

Of course, it didn't come about without a bit of controversy. Nearly a year earlier, Eddie Gold approached the Lancaster County Board for permission to remove a stone settee at the corner of 48th and O Streets. At the time, his

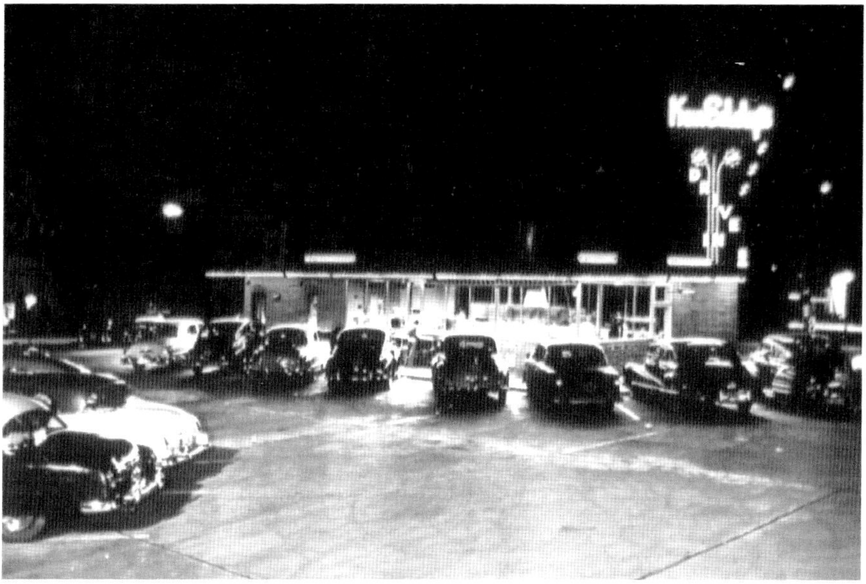

Founded by Eddie Gold in the late 1940s, Ken Eddys was a popular drive-in, as seen here at night near its opening, and later morphed into Eddy's Restaurant, a popular steakhouse and lounge. *Courtesy of Jim McKee.*

request drew opposition from the Lincoln Garden Club and the women's division of the Lincoln Chamber of Commerce.

"To me it looks hideous...it's just a heap of rock....[I]t didn't take much gray matter to plan it," he told the two groups at the meeting, according to the *Lincoln Star*.

A commissioner suggested that Eddie Gold, a Garden Club member and the county engineer meet to reach an agreement. A month later, the issue was back before the board, with county commissioners unanimously voting against Gold's request.

In early 1952, Ken Eddy's Drive-In began advertising for help. Gold and partner Kenneth Lydick had opened the restaurant together, but Gold bought out Lydick several months later. The drive-in served hamburgers, fries and shakes and soon became a popular hangout for all ages.

In February 1966, Gold closed Ken Eddy's for remodeling and, about three or four months later, reopened it as Eddy's Supper Club. Advertised in the newspaper as the "the new beautiful Eddy's Supper Club" with parking for two hundred cars, it enjoyed a "formal opening" in August, advertising three-dollar family and two-dollar non-resident memberships.

But the transition wasn't without controversy—this time a little more serious than a stone settee.

The previous summer, Eddie Gold had applied for a liquor license and received approval from the Nebraska Liquor Control Commission in September. The City of Lincoln, however, opposed the ruling and went to district court asking for a reversal.

The city alleged the commission's approval was contrary to and in violation of the Nebraska Liquor Control Act, which said no license could be granted to anyone who had been convicted of or pleaded guilty to gambling. Eddie Gold had been convicted of misdemeanors for running a gambling house prior to 1943, but he had had a clean record since. In February 1966, a district judge upheld the liquor commission's approval, paving the way for Gold to sell liquor at his new club.

Gold passed away in February 1970 at the age of sixty-one, leaving the restaurant to his wife, Lu Gold, to run. As Eddy's Restaurant, it became one of Lincoln's most popular steakhouses and lounges on the bustling O Street stretch that included Tony and Luigi's and the Legionnaire Club.

In 1980, Lu Gold told the *Lincoln Journal* that Eddy's brought three dining innovations to Lincoln: prime rib as a leading menu item, "two-fers" discount pricing for lounge patrons and special events for singles.

In April 1984, Lu Gold sold the restaurant to make way for new development, which included a grocery store (today's Super Saver). She told the *Lincoln Star* it wasn't on the market but decided to sell because of declining business: "I don't think the restaurant and bar business is the thing to be in today."

Prior to the reunion four years later, she stuck to her guns. "I don't miss the business," she told the *Lincoln Star*, "but I sure miss the people."

King's Food Host

Ask older diners what they remember most about eating at a King's Food Host, and you'll probably get a variety of answers.

For some, it was the burgers—those hand-pattied morsels featuring co-founder Larry Price's secret ingredient: "lots of pepper."

For others, it was the cheese frenchee, as much a Nebraska product as Runza, Kool-Aid and the Vise Grip. The frenchee may have been nothing more than bread, mayonnaise, cheese and sometimes tuna dredged in cornflake crumbs and deep fried, but it was delicacy of sorts that remains a favorite menu item at Amigo's/King Classic and Don & Millie's.

And for a few others, it may have been the telephone ordering system, first implemented at the original King's in Bethany. Diners would request burgers, frenchees, onion rings, fries and more via tabletop telephones, and as you can imagine, many parents heard the words "I wanna do it" from their children when it came time to order.

Those memories were because of Price, who started it all with a burger stand in 1934 at the Nebraska State Fair. Then seventeen, Price already was a food-service "veteran," having begun his career at age eight, selling vegetables door to door. At thirteen, he had his first retail outlet—a soda pop stand he ran with his cousins at the corner of 27th and O Streets.

Just out of high school, Price approached state fair officials about running a hamburger stand, but was told "no" because all the permits had been granted. Just as Price was about to leave, a man withdrew from his spot. Price borrowed a cookie sheet, spatula and kerosene stove and began the

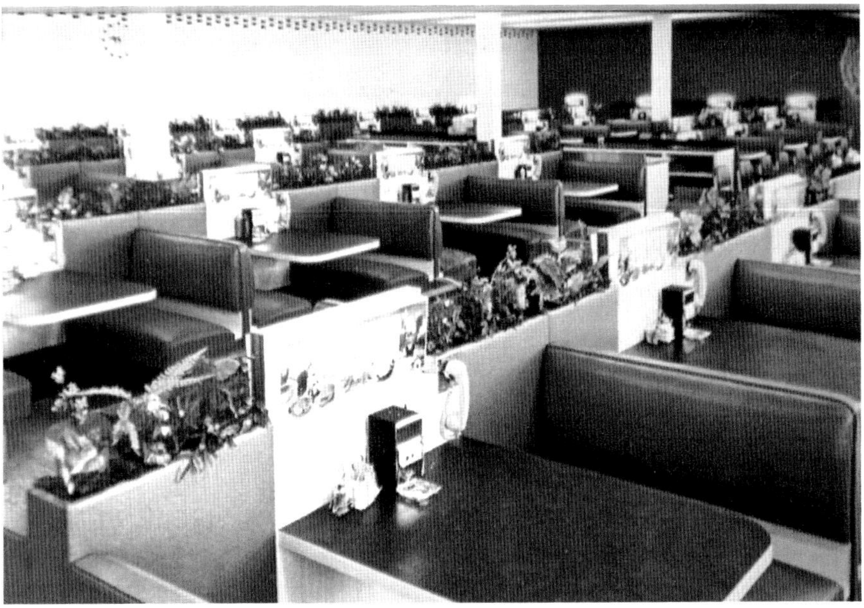

King's featured telephones at booths to call in orders to the kitchen like these seen at the location at 48th and O Streets. *Courtesy of Jim McKee.*

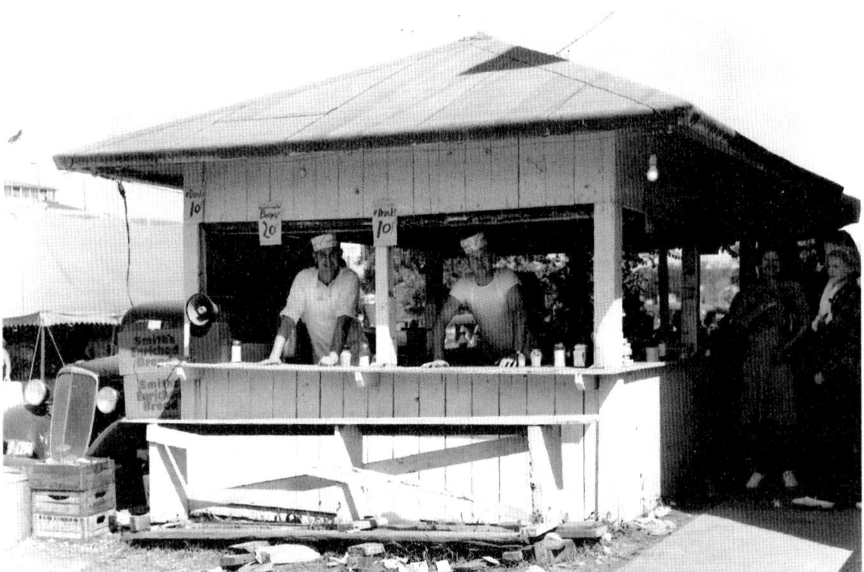

King's Food Host operates at the Nebraska State Fair in 1946. *Courtesy Jim McKee.*

Topper sandwich stand, so named, according to Lincoln historian Jim McKee, because Price boasted his hamburgers couldn't be topped.

After graduating from Nebraska Wesleyan and serving in the army, Price coached basketball at his alma mater, worked as a policeman, rebuilt houses in Bethany and operated a grocery store at 1551 North Cotner Boulevard. In 1949, he opened Toppers Restaurant in an abandoned gas station at 1340 North Cotner Boulevard.

As McKee noted in one of his newspaper columns, Price's timing was impeccable. Cars and fast food were becoming popular in the city. In 1955, Price partnered with Jim, who had been a salesman at Gold's department store, to form King's Drive-In Restaurant at the Toppers location. It became known for its bright-orange booths, telephone ordering and no smoking policy.

"I am not crusading against the cigarette, but I don't want to make it easy for the teenager to break the law," Price told the *Lincoln Star* in 1964.

Price and King continued their partnership until 1960, which by then included restaurants at 19th and O, 40th and South and a buffet at 13th and North. When the partnership amicably dissolved, King retained the 40th and South outlet and, in 1962, opened another store at 10th and South Streets. He called them Kingscrest Restaurants.

King's son, also named Jim, told McKee the two men decided to go their separate ways because Price wanted to franchise and expand, while King was concerned that doing so might affect the product's quality.

Price did expand. In 1964, he opened the twenty-second King's Food Host at 4701 O Street. The site also included a training facility, general office, kitchen and catering facility with a $500,000 budget.

"Our business is really people," Price told the *Lincoln Star* prior to the store's open house. "If we have good employees with ability to manage themselves, to command earned respect, this is what King's Food Hosts needs to be successful."

By the following year, the chain had grown to 45 locations. In a column, McKee noted those 45 stores used ten tons of beef a week, baked three hundred pies a day and had several women doing nothing but making the signature frenchees. At its peak, there were nearly 140 King's restaurants in seventeen states and Canada.

Price sold the restaurant chain in 1972, and soon after, it fell into bankruptcy. The number of stores dwindled. The last one bearing the King's name in Lincoln, at 923 South Street, closed in February 2001. Months earlier, the one at 1650 Cornhusker Highway closed.

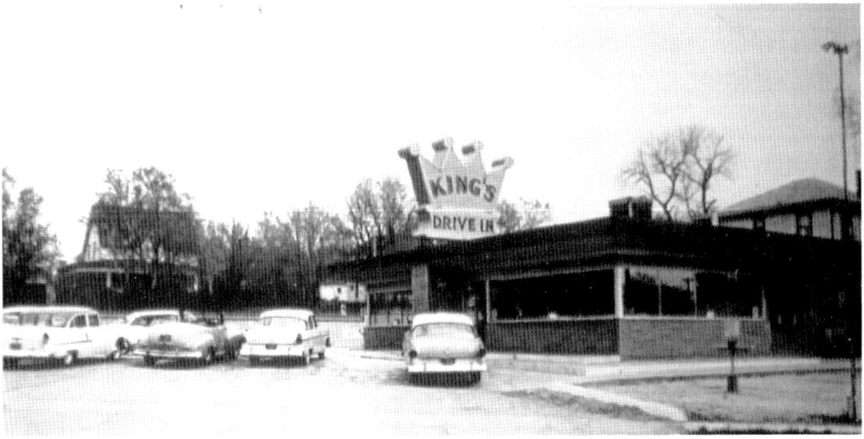

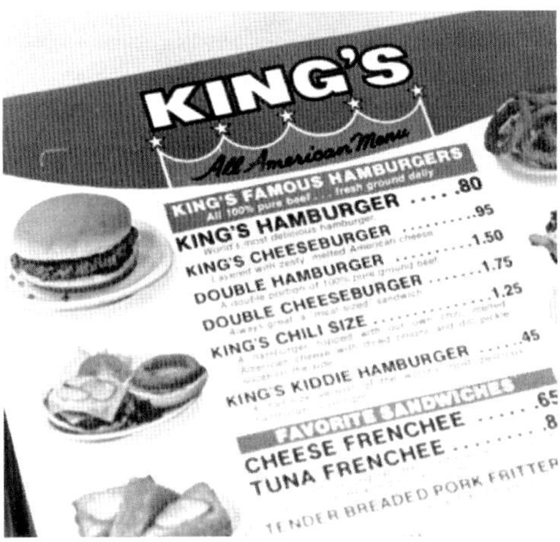

Above: King's had drive-ins throughout Lincoln, including this one in 1959 at 66th Street and North Cotner Boulevard. *Courtesy of Jim McKee.*

Left: King's "All American Menu" from 1974 included the drive-in's famous burgers and cheese frenchees. *Courtesy of the* Lincoln Journal Star.

After King's, Price turned to local projects, including two Lincoln Pantry restaurants—building the Bethany Pantry for his brother Joe on the site of the original King's—Van Dorn Plaza shopping center, the Cotner Center for Living, the Stuart Building renovation and North Gate Garden Estates senior condominiums.

But he didn't leave burgers completely behind. Over the years, he returned to the state fair to operate a restaurant in Agricultural Hall, often frying the burgers himself. A photo of him at the grill graced the front page of the *Lincoln Star* in February 1983. Price died of a heart attack on August 28, 1999, at the age of eighty-three.

King's returned in 2003. That's when Amigo's began selling such King's staples as the burgers and cheese frenchees under the Amigo's/King's Classic name.

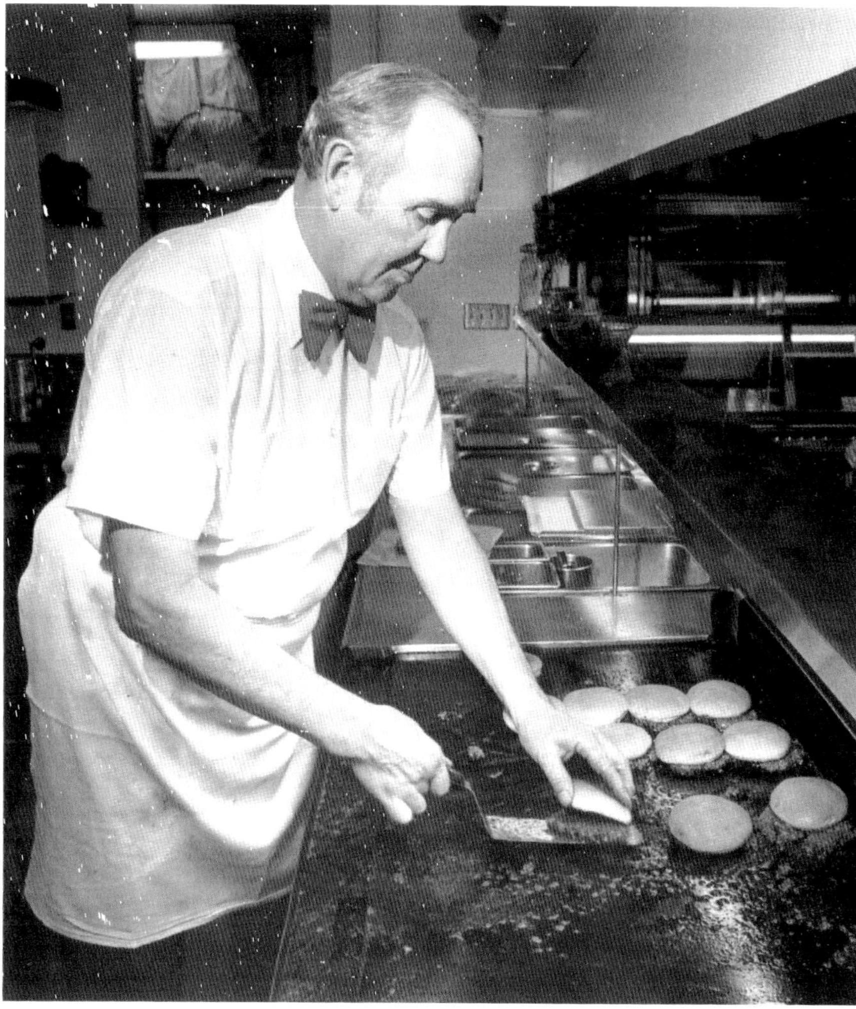

King's Food Host co-founder Larry Price grills burgers in February 1983. *Courtesy of the Lincoln Journal Star.*

King's Cheese Frenchee

In 1985, Bethany Pantry, owned by Joe Price, brother of King's Food Host co-founder Larry Price, shared the recipe for the much-loved cheese frenchee with the *Lincoln Star*. Larry Price created the sandwich just before the Lenten season in 1958 after experimenting with several kinds of fish sandwiches and even a hot peanut butter sandwich.

1 ½ cups milk
2 eggs
½ cup powdered cheese
Miracle Whip
8 slices of bread
4 slices of American cheese
2 cups cracker meal

Mix together milk, eggs and powdered cheese to make egg batter. Spread Miracle Whip generously over each slice of bread. Sandwich each slice of cheese between two slices of bread. Cut sandwiches into quarter, dip in egg batter to moisten and roll in cracker meal. Deep fry at about 360 degrees until golden brown. For best results, use bread that's at least a day old and fresh oil. Makes 4 sandwiches.

—Chef's Corner, the *Lincoln Star*, April 17, 1985

Kuhl's Restaurant

Menu items at Kuhl's Restaurant were created in-house, with one notable exception: the Kuhlburger. The credit for that one goes to Lincoln banker T.B. Strain, who was regular at the downtown Lincoln restaurant.

Pearl Kuhl said Strain came in one day with a special order. He wanted a double hamburger cooked medium well with chopped onions and American cheese stuck between the patties.

"Today you call them stuffed burgers," Pearl said. "Everyone has one now."

But in the 1970s, it was unique. So impressed with how Kuhl's made it, Strain suggested the restaurant add it to the menu. Maybe other hungry diners would like to enjoy it, too.

"He said to call it whatever we wanted, so we called it a Kuhlburger," Pearl said. "He was a gem. We had some marvelous customers. A lot of our customers became close personal friends."

Pearl and Kurt A. Kuhl operated Kuhl's Restaurant from 1968 to 1985 at 1038 O Street, but they were a part of Lincoln's restaurant scene long before that. The couple even met at a restaurant. Kurt, who was from Coleridge, came to Lincoln after World War II and landed a job at Western Electric. Pearl was a waitress at Nix Steakhouse at 17th and Van Dorn Streets.

"He started eating at the restaurant because he lived nearby," Pearl said. "That's how I got acquainted with him. He kept hanging around and wouldn't go home."

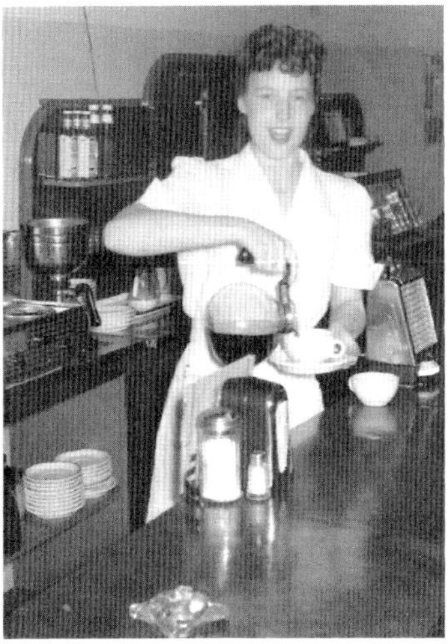

Pearl Kuhl works as a server at Nix Steakhouse. *Courtesy of Pearl Kuhl.*

Pearl worked nine years at Nix. Legendary late-night TV talk show host Johnny Carson, then a student at the University of Nebraska, dined there often with his fraternity brothers, Pearl said.

"He was kind of...OK, you know," Pearl said. "When you saw him on television, that was kind of the way he was. He was nice."

In June 1951, Pearl and Kurt married. In 1955, they bought Nix and renamed it Kuhl's Steak House.

"She couldn't bear to leave it, so she twisted my arm until we bought it and that's how we got in the restaurant business," Kurt told the *Lincoln Journal* in 1983. "My arm is still sore."

The steakhouse became a hit, especially with Irving Junior High School students, who were allowed to venture off campus during lunch. Kuhl's premade the burgers, packaged them with french fries and had them ready to go.

"We had this one young boy who always wanted to come and open the pop," Pearl said. "That was when pop was in bottles, and we had a cooler of ice with the bottles in it and the pop bottle opener on the outside. He was always opening the pop for the kids as they lined up to get their hamburgers and French fries."

That young man was Bob Felber, and "he hung around so long, he started working with us," Pearl said. "He stayed with us until O Street."

There were stops in between Kuhl's Steak House and Kuhl's Restaurant for the Kuhls. Pearl said they closed the steakhouse in 1960 after the city built a nearby fire station, which "took a lot of the parking off the street."

In the summer of 1960, the Kuhls took over one of Mike Tillman's restaurants, the one in Rathbone Village at Winthrop Road and South Streets, and renamed it the Village Plaza. The restaurant is remembered for its basement party room called "The Cave." It was decorated like a cave, with walls resembling rocks and waitresses wearing cave uniforms.

After three years, Lincoln businessman Bennett Martin came calling, asking the Kuh's, first, to run the restaurant at the Capital Hotel at 11th and P Streets and later at the Lincoln Hotel at Ninth and P Streets. Martin eventually sold both parties, with the Capital Hotel becoming the downtown YMCA.

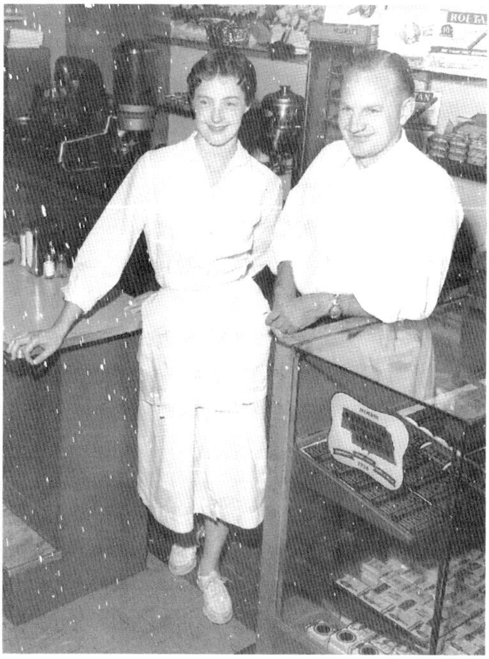

Left: Pearl and Kurt Kuhl stand inside of Kuhl's Steak House at 17th and Van Dorn Streets sometime in the late 1950s. *Courtesy of Pearl Kuhl.*

Below: Kuhl's Steak House featured tablecloths, placemats and fresh flowers at each table during its run from 1955 to 1960 at 17th and Van Dorn Streets. *Courtesy of Pearl Kuhl.*

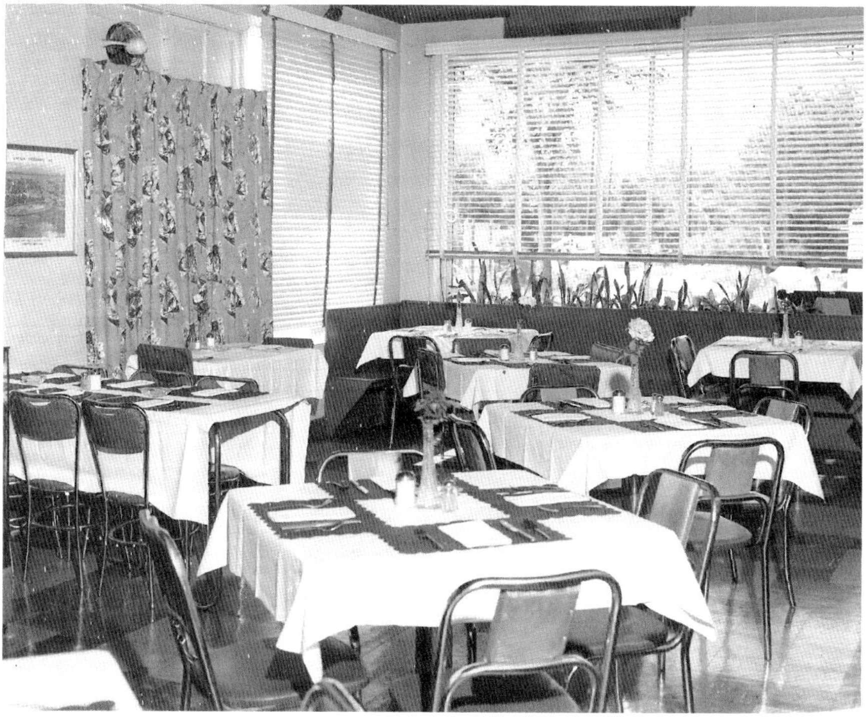

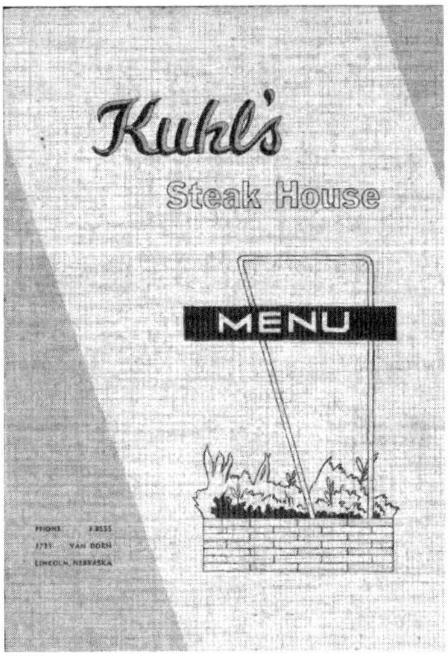

The cover of the menu from Kuhl's Steak House, which operated form from 1955 to 1960 at 17th and Van Dorn Streets. *Courtesy of Pearl Kuhl.*

"We joked that when they start putting the swimming pool in our kitchen, that's when we would have to leave there," Pearl said.

On February 12, 1968, the Kuhls opened Kuhl's Restaurant at 1038 O Street, offering home-style favorites from 7:00 a.m. to 8:00 p.m. Monday through Saturday in a dining room, that, with its paneled walls, looked more like a home than a restaurant.

"We're kind of unique—and I don't think too many restaurants can say this—in that there are people who eat with us three times a day," Kurt told the *Lincoln Journal* in 1983.

Said Pearl: "I really liked downtown. I like O Street. I really did. It was a wonderful location. We had marvelous neighbors. We had a lot of customers from the businesses up and down O Street."

Like many restaurants, Kuhl's was a family operation. When they were young, sons Kurt J. and Paul worked alongside their father in the kitchen, while Pearl worked the floor and baked the pies—apple, cherry, pumpkin, mince.

"I think the best times for my husband was when the three of them worked on football Saturdays," Pearl said.

The Kuhls sold the restaurant in 1985 when Kurt's health began to fail. He died in 2013 at the age of ninety.

The transition was seamless. Greek immigrants Pete and Stella Hametis came to Lincoln from Carroll, Iowa, where they worked a Bonanza restaurant. Pete was looking for his own business when he learned Kuhl's was for sale. The couple kept the name, much of the menu—adding some Greek entrees, of course—and the look because of the restaurant's superb reputation. Why fix something that isn't broken?

Stella greeted and seated customers, calling many of them "sweetie," "honey" or "Miss America," and Pete, with his horn-rimmed glasses perched atop his head, became a familiar sight at the kitchen window. Stella did add a personal touch to the restaurant. Family pictures filled up the wall behind the cash register. Like the Kuhls before them, the Hametises employed their children, making it a true "family" restaurant.

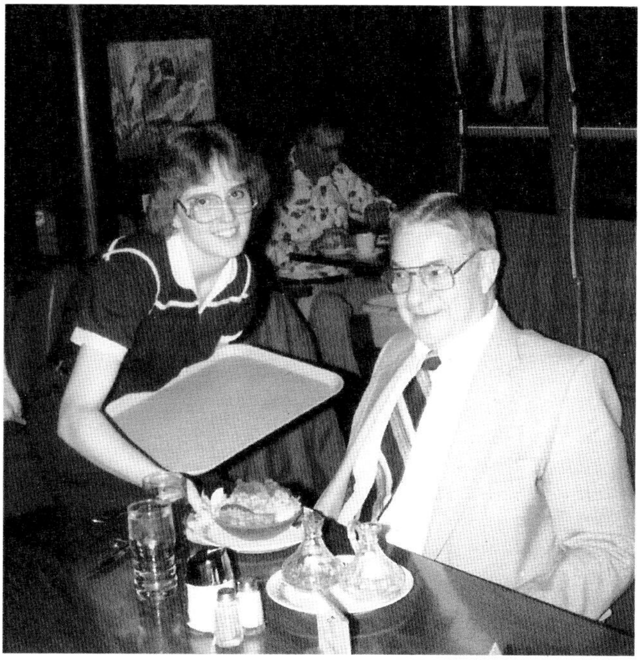

A server waits on a customer at Kuhl's Restaurant at 1038 O Street. *Courtesy of Pearl Kuhl.*

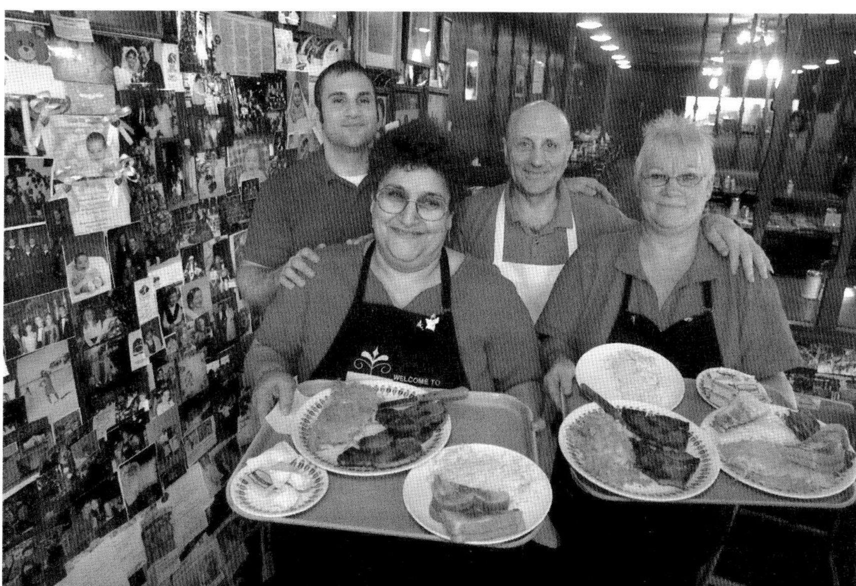

Stella and Pete Hametis with son Jim (*left*) and server Mary Styskal (*right*) show off some of the food served in February 2005 at Kuhl's Restaurant. The Hametis family operated Kuhl's from 1985 to 2007. The pictures and clippings at left highlight news and events in the lives of customers and family members. *Courtesy of the* Lincoln Journal Star.

But after twenty-three years, the Hametises closed Kuhl's in March 2008 following a dispute with their landlord. The couple elected to retire instead of reopening Kuhl's elsewhere.

"For us, this was not only a business," Stella told the *Lincoln Journal Star*. "We had no time to socialize. We did it here. This was our life."

On its last day, a five-paragraph thank-you note from the Hametises hung from the front door.

"...We stuck together and fought to make it against all the odds and stayed at the top of our game until the very end," it read. "As much as we wish it would last forever, it's time to say goodbye."

Kuhl's Kuhlburger

2 ⅓-pound hamburger patties
Onion, finely chopped
American cheese slices
Salt and pepper, to taste

Sprinkle one patty with onion and cover with a slice of cheese. Top with the second patty and pinch to seal the edges. Salt and pepper to taste. Grill to medium well. Serve on a toasted bun.

—Courtesy of Pearl Kuhl

Lebsack Brothers Tavern

In 1985, Barrymore's, a bar in downtown Lincoln, attempted to replicate the chili served at Lebsack Brothers Tavern, with Barrymore's owner Jim Haberlan telling the *Lincoln Journal* at the time that "the trick is getting the right amount of grease, for lack of a better word."

Oh, that grease.

Diners like Haberlan, who had begun eating Lebsack's chili as college students, fondly remembered the grease. He said, "A lot of guys would order it with extra grease. You could order it with extra grease or light on the grease. But we haven't gotten that sophisticated yet."

Many Lincoln restaurants and cafés had their signature dishes. At Lebsack's, it was the chili, perfected by brothers John, Hank and Eddie Lebsack. Well, as the story goes, John actually gets the credit for the chili.

"John came up with the bean soup and chili," Eddie told legendary *Lincoln Journal* reporter and tavern regular Jim Raglin in 1974. "Hank made up the vegetable soup. I provide a lot of lip and guff. And I'm never wrong—until I get caught."

Part of the chili's appeal was the man serving it. The colorful Eddie Lebsack worked the room the way a stand-up comic does a microphone from the stage, tossing packages of oyster crackers to diners from his trademark carpenter apron. You didn't, according to Raglin, dare ask for more of them.

"I've got my opinions on lots of things, and I don't mind sharing them," Eddie said in 1974.

The tavern's roots date back to midnight on August 10, 1933, when Hank and John headed the line to get a beer license. It was the day Prohibition officially ended. The café eventually became known as Nebraska's oldest beer dispenser. Eddie joined his brothers in 1945 after service in World War II and continued to run the place following their deaths.

Hank and John opened the first store at Third and F Streets. The tavern moved three times over its forty-five-year history, to 719 P Street, 1126 P Street and, finally, in April 1972, to 220 North 10th Street, where it remained until Eddie sold it in September 1978 to Ogea, Don and Jek Kelly, who renamed it O.G. Kelly's.

In writing about the tavern's sale, which came off more like an obituary, Raglin opined: "Never ones to feature decor, the Lebsack boys put their talents into more important things, such as their chili, veg and bean soup, roast beef and a unique atmosphere that belonged to the customers as to the Lebsacks."

Eddie died on February 1, 1983, at age seventy-four, but the memory of the café he and his brothers created lives on, especially the chili, grease and all.

Maggie's Vegetarian Café

Maggie Pleskac began eating vegetarian in high school, never realizing that one day it would lead her to running what would arguably become Lincoln's most successful vegetarian restaurant.

The change came after after she read John Robbins's 1987 book *Diet for a New America*, which advocated for a plant-based vegan diet. The EarthSave founder also offered his views on the meat and dairy industries, world hunger and human health.

"When I read the book, it totally changed everything," Pleskac said.

> *I grew up in a farm family. I just assumed all meat was that pure. The whole family got together and butchered. This is what they did. Then they put the meat in the freezer. Coming from that background, I assumed all meat was like that.*
>
> [The book] *was my eye-opener. How do you feed a nation that's demanding this much quantity? Well, yeah, you have to go into factory farming. Once I learned about factory farming, that's what changed.*

She laughed thinking back about her decision, saying her heart was in the right place, but her stomach not so much.

"I was so unhealthy when I first started," Pleskac said. "It was the worst vegetarian diet imaginable. I just simply omitted meat, so I would go through the drive-thru at Runza and get the fries and the onion dip. I would go through Amigo's, and I would get the cheesy [burrito] with a side of ranch. I probably ate worse when I became a vegetarian than when I was eating meat."

Then she landed her first job at Open Harvest, a cooperative in south Lincoln known for its produce, deli and health food selection. Pleskac worked in the deli, eventually becoming manager and developing recipes.

"Open Harvest was this eye-opener of spices," she said. "When I first came into the deli, we were using the *Moosewood Cookbook* by Mollie Katzan. A lot of those recipes had so much spice to them, so it was really, for me, a flavor opener. That's what I had been missing from the palate. There was so much stimulation on the palate, I never craved anything else."

Pleskac worked off and on over the five years at Open Harvest, taking a year off to study in the Netherlands and another year to work at a co-op in Arizona. She had planned to leave Arizona for California, but a relationship she was in turned sour and she returned to her Lincoln hometown and Open Harvest.

That's when she realized that "everything I was doing there, I could do on my own."

Pleskac started with a "test market," opening a booth with roommate Carlee Shearman at the Haymarket Farmers Market. They called it "Lovin' From the Oven" and offered baked goods, ranging from focaccia bread to mini-loaves of carrot cake and banana bread to vegan muffins.

"We had a following," Pleskac said. "People really wanted the vegan muffins. Vegan baking…that was about the time it really took. People really wanted this."

In July 2000, at age twenty-five, she opened Maggie's Vegetarian Cafe at 311 North Eighth Street in Lincoln's Haymarket. With the help of her father, Michael, and mother, Doris, she created a quaint café featuring exposed brick, pastel lime-green walls and seating for about ten.

Her menu consisted of wraps—roasted veggie, avocado, three-cheese, baked falafel—and a variety of "plates" such as nut meat tacos and a Southwest black bean casserole. She baked more muffins and cookies and offered a daily soup. Her foods contained the freshest, organic ingredients. She didn't cut corners.

"People wanted something different, something new," Pleskac said. "People want real fresh food. They want the description that they read on the menu to be real. They read that on the menu and it sounds amazing. They want amazing."

Food Network Magazine named Maggie's avocado wrap, which featured her homemade herb mustard dressing, Nebraska's sandwich to try in a fifty-state survey. It was the café's top seller.

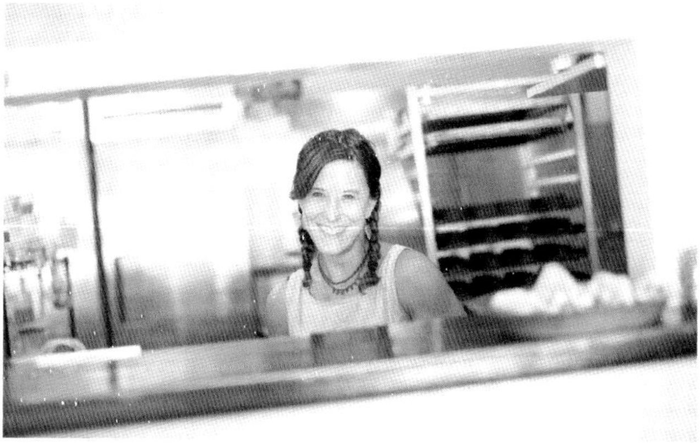
Maggie Pleskac operated Maggie's Vegetarian Cafe for seventeen and a half years in the Haymarket. It was arguably the city's most successful vegetarian and vegan eatery. *Dana Damewood for New Prairie Kitchen.*

"Which I think is funny because we pride ourselves on local and here we have avocados, which we obviously can't grow here," she said, laughing.

Just about everything else she sourced locally, getting fresh produce, cheeses and more from such suppliers as Robinette Farms, Shadowbrook and Common Good. A wood sign with the words "know your farmer know your food" hung on one of the café's walls.

"I can't say enough about the relationship we had with our farmers," Pleskac said.

After her first year, Pleskac paid back half her debt. The second year she was debt-free, and by the third year, she had begun turning a profit. She expected none of it.

"I didn't want to be home," she admitted. "I was on my way to California. That was my intention. I thought if I'm back here, I'm just going to open a café. If it doesn't work, then I'm back on track to move out to California. I had no idea the response was going to be what it was."

It was tremendous—with vegetarians and non-vegetarians.

"Half of our customers were not vegetarian," Pleskac said. "It was just food that they enjoyed. Honestly, it's how you felt after you ate there. It's a cleaner, lighter feeling. You don't go back to your office and fall asleep. It's clean food. Nothing's fried. It's not oily. And it's sourced local, most of it."

After five years, she began to shoot for ten and this fifteen. She married and gave birth to two beautiful daughters. At year fifteen, she decided she had enough. Tragedy struck. Her husband, Pat Clinch, died after losing his battle with pancreatic cancer.

"I was totally done at fifteen, but everybody said I couldn't make a big financial decision until two years after the death," she said. "That's what everybody advised me. I was pretty sure I was done. I had been done."

On December 31, 2017, Pleskac closed her store after seventeen and a half years, saying it was "time to reset." She thanked her customers on Facebook.

"When I opened Maggie's Café in July 2000, I wasn't sure that Lincoln was ready to support a vegan/vegetarian café," she wrote. "Not only was the community ready for plant-based fare but also longing for fresh, organic, locally sourced foods. For the past 17+ years, we have served the need for real food."

When she's ready, Pleskac said she'll return to Lincoln's restaurant scene. She loves food. She loves talking about food.

"Tony and Luigi's…I remember getting the little palate cleanser between your courses," she said with heavy sigh. "Somebody needs to do that again. And it even wasn't that much. It was like a melon-baller, [but] it was just enough. That one little thing just upped the ante of everything for that whole experience. That's what I always say….That's what turned me on to the restaurant industry those details that T and L always had."

Maggie's Spicy Hummus

2 cups chickpeas
½ cup lemon juice
1 tablespoon cumin seed powder
8 garlic cloves
1 teaspoon salt
½ cup chopped onions
½ teaspoon cayenne pepper
½ teaspoon black pepper
⅓ cup tahini

In a blender or food processor, blend together chickpeas, lemon juice, cumin seed powder, garlic cloves, salt, onions, cayenne pepper and black pepper. Add tahini to make creamy. Add water to thin, if desired.

—Courtesy of Maggie Pleskac, Maggie's Vegetarian Café

Miller & Paine Tea Room

Our conversation began with servings of Miller & Paine's famous cinnamon rolls and ended with clean plates.

Enjoying a cinnamon roll only seemed appropriate as Bob Campbell, Miller & Paine president and CEO, discussed the store's tearoom and the significance it held for Lincoln's dining scene from the time the store opened in 1915.

The fifth-floor tearoom, as many know, was known for its chicken pot pies, macaroni and cheese and cinnamon rolls. Today, Runza, the Lincoln-founded and based fast-food chain, owns the rights to many of those recipes, including those delicious cinnamon rolls.

"I know Arne Pederson used lard," Campbell said of Miller & Paine's longtime bakery manager.

> *I'm not sure if Runza's using lard, but lard was important to it. Lard and butter. Arne would prepare those the day before and let those set up overnight.*
>
> *Each strip was cut and basted with butter and cinnamon and rolled and then put in the pan and allowed to rise. The next day he would add more cinnamon and sugar mixture on the top and bake and it would caramelize to an extent. He was a master at making those.*

Indeed, he was.

In 2007, at age eighty-six, Pederson prepared some for me. I was at his home—greeted by the fragrance of cinnamon as they baked in the

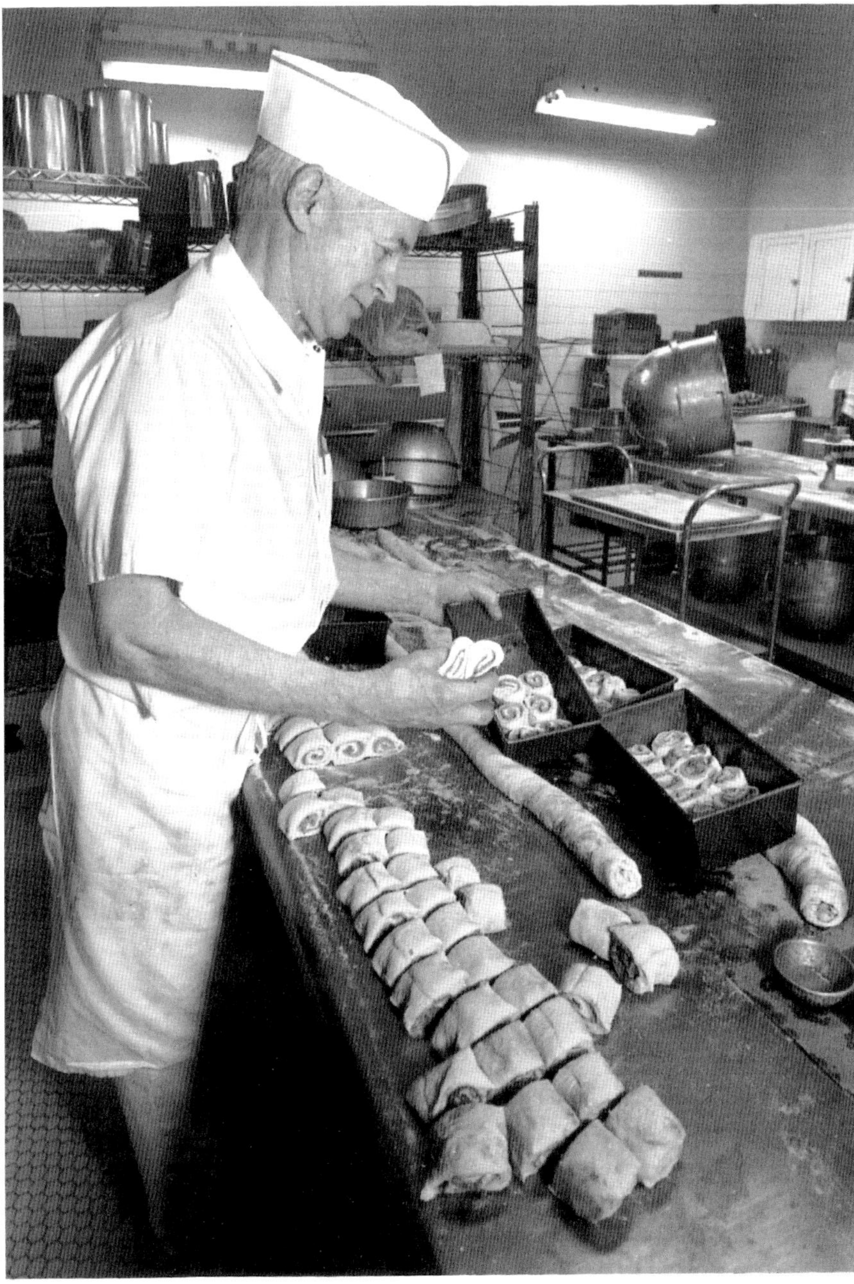

Miller & Paine's Arne Pederson places cinnamon rolls in pans for baking in January 1986. *Courtesy of the* Lincoln Journal Star.

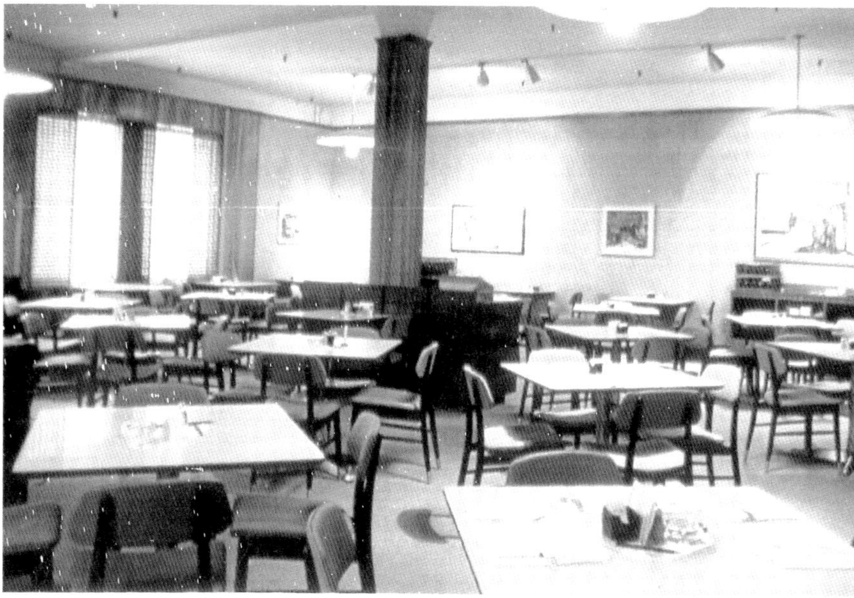

The Miller & Paine Tea Room, located on the department store's fifth floor, drew Lincoln business leaders, office workers and shoppers with a menu featuring freshly baked cinnamon rolls, macaroni and cheese and chicken pot pies. *Courtesy of Jim McKee.*

oven, while still on the front step—to profile Pederson for the the *Lincoln Journal Star*.

These rolls were legendary. Many of us savored them with our parents or grandparents in the department store. Many more drove miles to purchase them, buying dozens at a time to carry us over until our next trip to the capital city.

Campbell's great-grandfather was Miller & Paine co-founder John Miller. And though no one knows for sure, Campbell believed the recipe came to Lincoln from Pennsylvania with the Miller family in the late 1800s.

"There's more to the recipe than just ingredients," Campbell said in 2007. "It's about how to make them. Arne really has it down."

Indeed, he did.

That's why people often approached him for the recipe, which outside of a few close friends and family, he didn't share. "I hear that [request] all the time," Pederson said at the time.

He then recalled the time he saw a recipe for the rolls in the *Journal Star*. A reader, claiming to have worked at Miller & Paine, was sharing it with other readers.

"I laughed and almost called him," Pederson told me. "He had cake mix in there. A box of cake mix. I couldn't believe it. It would make a tasty roll, but there is no cake mix in the [M&P] cinnamon roll at all."

And though he didn't share the recipe with me, he offered hints as to why the rolls taste so good. The cinnamon, for instance, was from Saigon, only available through a company in Evanston, Illinois. It cost about twice as much as normal cinnamon, he said. Bakers shouldn't cut corners. Frozen bread was a definite no-no. Pederson made his dough from scratch, letting it rise an hour before knocking it down, letting it rest and rise for another twenty minutes.

"There's where your flavor is developed," he said.

When Miller & Paine put the rolls on sale, the bakery would go through one thousand dozen per day, Pederson said in 2007. That wasn't enough.

"We gave rain checks," he said. "It would take three weeks for us to catch up."

The department store received orders for them from all over the country, even from as far away as Australia. And when Nebraska played home football games…

"I had to have 200 dozen sitting at the case when the store opened," Pederson said. "People from towns around Lincoln would take 40 or 50 dozen at a time. They took orders for other people."

Campbell said he believed the Miller & Paine Tea Room opened at or close to the same time the department store did in 1915. It occupied the top floor of the five-story building across the alley from Miller & Paine's eight-story building at 13th and O Streets. The room was intended to showcase the store's ever-growing art collection, which featured local painters, some of whom, like Terrence Duren, became nationally prominent.

"It was done primarily for the shoppers," Campbell said. "It had a great following. Ladies would have hats and white gloves. It was quite a time in the twenties and even into the thirties when these department stores were flourishing all over the country. There were a number like Miller & Paine—smaller regional or local department stores, mostly family-owned businesses."

John Miller, who began in business in Lincoln in 1879, partnered with investor Dr. Bartlett L. Paine, first on a four-story store in 1889 and then on the Miller & Paine complex. Campbell said Miller patterned Miller & Paine after large Chicago and New York department stores but on a smaller scale.

"Most of them had food service," Campbell said. "Most of them had tearooms like this."

Lunch became its primary purpose, with service clubs, bride groups and Lincoln's business leaders meeting over the noon hour. The business leaders had their own "men's table," surrounded by red upholstered chairs.

"Finally, in the 1970s, we established a women's table as well," Campbell said. "We finally got politically correct. [Those tables] were amazing. Those people would be up there. It was a great time for leaders of the community to get together and visit over lunch."

The menu featured typical lunch fare—sandwiches, soups, salads, pastries—but everything was made from scratch.

"The chicken pot pie…a lot of people will say 'Gee, I remember it had peas in it,'" Campbell said.

> *No, to my knowledge, it never had peas in it. It may have been a Gold's chicken pot pie they were remembering. It was generous amounts of chicken in it and potatoes and this wonderful chicken gravy. They used this particular kind of, I think, stewing hen, very fatty, very rich. And they made this deep, rich, yellow gravy. It was wonderful. It's amazing so many of us have survived this long. It was cholesterol heaven. It was a great product and a favorite for many, many years.*

In July 1988, Miller & Paine sold to Dillard's but retained its restaurant, bakery, candy and fur storage businesses. Dillard's left after two years, and Miller & Paine eventually divested itself of the remaining businesses. The Miller & Paine Tea Room served its last meal to the public on February 8, 1991.

The cinnamon rolls disappeared, too, but resurfaced in 1997 at Cinnamon Central, which had acquired the rights to them and sold them at area grocery stores. But the bakery closed, and again, the rolls were gone. In February 2007, Runza acquired the rights and began baking and selling them at its stores.

The Mug

Albert Benjamin Nebelsick may not be as well known as Ray Kroc of McDonald's fame or Wendy's founder Dave Thomas, but he holds a special place in Lincoln dining history. As owner of the Mug, the popular drive-in of the 1930s and '40s, Nebelsick pioneered the fast-food movement in the capital city.

Incorporated in 1930 by Lincoln businessmen Chester E. Ager, R.A. Russell and Dr. Carl Kail, the Mug opened first as a root beer stand, making its home on the southwest corner of 33rd and O Streets.

The Mug couldn't be missed; its principal structure was a tall cylindrical tower built to represent a root beer mug—only it had a face. Near its top, the tower had large illuminated eyes that moved from side to side. A huge nose protruded halfway down, and near its base, a dispensing counter formed a long mouth, with teeth marked on and above the opening.

It was something to behold.

Nebelsick took over the Mug around 1933, a couple of years after acquiring the Dutch Mill on the southeast corner of Cotner Boulevard and O street. Like the Mug, the Dutch Mill was unique in its look. Built by Holland Lumber Co. in 1927, the Dutch Mill was designed (and first operated) by J.V. Robinson as a Dutch windmill, complete with huge fan blades.

That Nebelsick purchased the Dutch Mill and the Mug came as no surprise considering his background.

A native of Owensville, Missouri, Nebelsick had worked for the Postal Telegraph Co. in Lincoln from 1919 to 1934. Unemployed during the

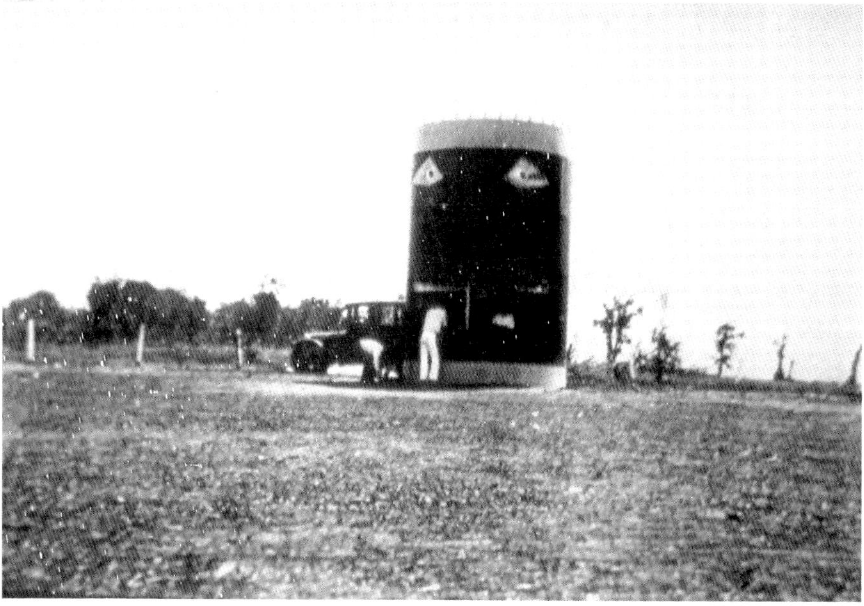

The Mug, as seen here circa 1930s, operated at 33rd and O Streets. The drive-in was built to resemble a mug with face on it, with illuminated "eyes" at the top that moved from side to side. *Courtesy of Jim McKee.*

Depression, he found work in rural southeastern Nebraska selling Watkins products. He also opened the Owl, a root beer stand, on South 14th Street between Stockwell and Burnham.

For additional income, Nebelsick sold carbon dioxide gas and root beer concentrate, supplied by the Dutch Mill, along his Watkins route. Of course, the Owl and the Mug used the concentrate.

After acquiring the Mug, Nebelsick grew its menu to include root beer floats, confections, sandwiches and coffee, thus becoming one of the earliest drive-ins in Lincoln. Servers wore white trousers, white shirts and black bow ties. The store became known for innovation, such as serving free four-ounce mugs of root beer to children accompanied by a paying adult.

The Mug operated into the mid-1950s. An auction for its equipment occurred on February 25, 1958.

Norma's Place

The sausage cheeseburger wasn't on the menu, but that didn't stop the customer from asking about it.

"You have these big sausage patties that look just like a hamburger," Leroy Latzel remembered the customer saying. "Can I have one of those with cheese on it on a bun?"

The answer, of course, was "yes."

"They knew if they came to our place, they could get what they wanted," said Norma Latzel, the café's namesake.

Norma's son Leroy agreed.

"If you wanted those little square potatoes in a stir fry, we made it," he said. "We could come up with a price for anything you wanted to eat."

That's how it was at Norma's Place, the small, neighborhood café known for its home-style food, fast service and friendly staff.

"It was a good experience," Leroy said. "It really was. There was a lot of nice people. It was just like a little town cafe."

Charles and Norma Latzel moved to Lincoln from Neligh in 1950 when Charles went to work for a building supply company. In the late 1960s, Norma landed a job, first as a bookkeeper, then a manger of a Lincoln truck stop.

After three years, she left and began working at Laurie's Cafe in Havelock, a northeast Lincoln neighborhood. A few months later, Norma and Charles purchased the café, opening Norma's Place in August 1972 at 6105 Havelock Avenue.

After working at the truck stop, "I pretty much knew what was what," Norma said. "I wanted to get out of there, so I found the one in Havelock and bought it."

Why Havelock?

"It was available and I was welcomed," Norma said.

"It's like a little hometown community out there," said Leroy, who worked for his mother and took over the café with his wife, Angie, in January 1994. "A lot of people in Havelock didn't even consider it to be a part of Lincoln."

With the motto "Always Good Food," Norma's operated from 5:00 a.m. to 8:00 p.m. weekdays and 5:00 a.m. to 2:00 p.m. on Saturday. It closed Sundays, but the family used that day to clean and prepare for the next week.

"People would ask 'When are you going to have meatloaf?' so every Sunday we would make out the [specials] board for the week," Leroy said.

The cafe served pan-fried chicken on Wednesdays. Meatloaf, chicken and noodles and tuna and noodles were among the daily specials. "All the stuff that makes you fat," Leroy joked.

But its signature dish was biscuits and gravy. The key ingredient: dried onions.

"They would come off the highway because people told them this was the place to come for biscuits and gravy," Norma said.

Norma's Place became as significant to the neighborhood as Misty's, Lincoln's legendary steakhouse, and the Isles, known for it "Leaning Tower of Pizza." As Norma's had only forty-six seats, it wasn't unusual for diners to share tables with strangers during busy lunches.

"That's how everybody formed friendships," Leroy said. "You don't see that everywhere. That's the whole deal behind the small-town café is most people get to know each other."

But Leroy admitted it became more challenging after Burger King opened a store at 5940 Havelock Avenue in the 1990s. To counter its presence, Norma's Place stepped up its game at lunchtime, he said.

"With our daily specials, they were prepared and ready to go," he said. "It was just a matter of dishing them up. Our waitresses were top notch. They would get the order in there, and Millie [Walker], our cook, she would put the food on the plate and out the window and 'slurp, slurp, slurp.' In fifteen minutes, there would be another person sitting there. That was the big thing.

"You could stand in line at Burger King for ten minutes to get your order taken. At Norma's, you've sat down and are out the door in the same amount of time."

Norma's Place celebrated its thirtieth anniversary with a party in August 2002. In May 2003, Leroy and Angie sold the restaurant. It was time to move

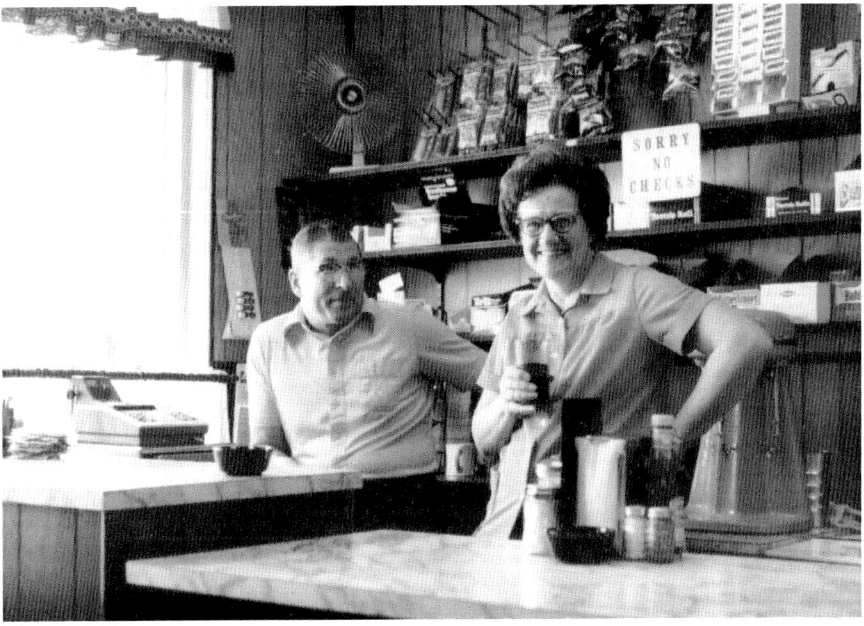

Charles and Norma Latzel opened Norma's Place at 6105 Havelock Avenue in August 1972. *Courtesy of Leroy Latzel.*

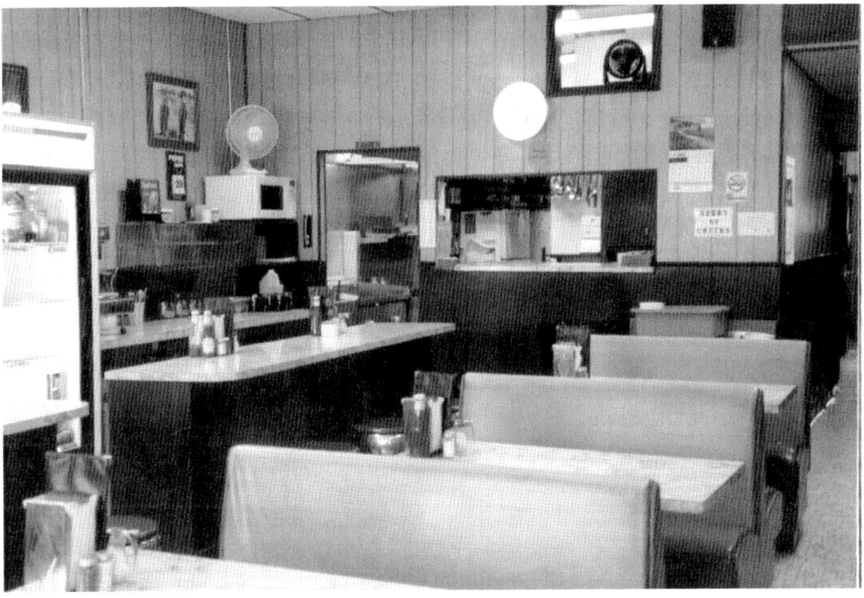

Norma's Place was a family-owned diner in Havelock known for its biscuits and gravy and daily lunch specials. *Courtesy of Leroy Latzel.*

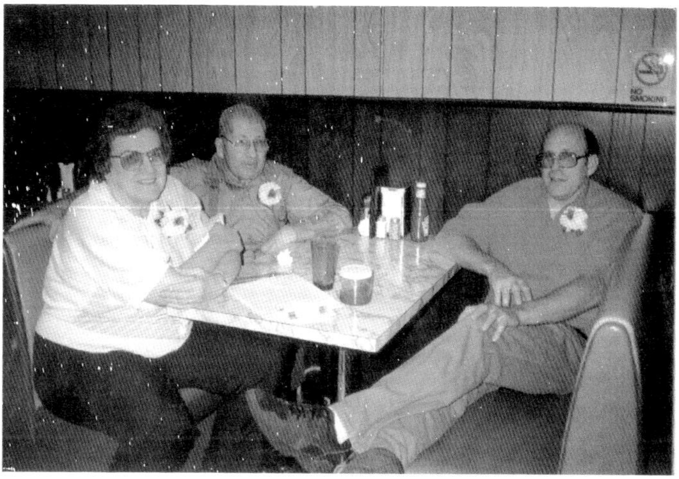

Norma, Charles and Leroy Latzel celebrate Norma's Place's thirtieth anniversary in 2002. The family sold the restaurant the following year. *Courtesy of Leroy Latzel.*

on and do other things, said Leroy, who also was a cabinetmaker. The café continued for a short time under two more owners before closing for good.

Norma's husband, Charles, who loved to tinker around the café, building, in one instance, a device to marry catsup bottles, died in September 2003.

Norma said she cherishes the memories. Today, she dines at Virginia's Travelers Cafe, another north Lincoln institution, where she sees some of her former customers.

"I don't miss the work," she said, "but I miss the people."

Norma's Place's Sausage Gravy

¾ of a 5-pound sausage roll
1 to 1 ½ cups dried onion (or a ¼ of the jar)
½ cup garlic salt
Pie tin full of flour
2 gallons milk

Brown sausage. Add dried onion and garlic salt. Do not discard the grease. Add flour and milk and stir until thick. The restaurant prepared large batches to serve its breakfast crowd. This recipe serves 50 or more, so it'll take some experimentation for smaller batches.

—Courtesy of Norma Latzel, Norma's Place

Papa John's

Considering that they immigrated from a Greek island, it may seem obvious why John and Despina Kazas opened a Greek restaurant in downtown Lincoln.

But John Kazas was a steak-and-potato man, and if he had his druthers, Papa John's would have been a steak-and-potato kind of restaurant.

But he didn't. And so it wasn't—initially.

"I couldn't do American food," he said in an interview at the Parthenon, the successful restaurant that his sons George and Mike operate in southeast Lincoln. "I couldn't sell steak because I had a non-compete with Bonanza. I couldn't sell any red meat or anything that had to do with a steakhouse for five years. For that reason, I had no choice."

So in 1989, after five years running a Bonanza in Cairo, Iowa, and another six years operating one in Lincoln, he and Despina opened Papa John's as a Greek restaurant at 114 South 14th Street.

"I got tired of franchises, of working for other people" Kazas told me in 2000 when I reviewed his restaurant for the *Lincoln Journal Star*. "I wanted to work for myself. Getting involved in Papa John's was the best thing that I ever did."

Papa, in his trademark red apron, along with Mrs. K, introduced many thankful Lincoln diners to Greek cuisine, from moussaka (an eggplant casserole) to souvlaki (a marinated pork, chicken, beef or lamb kabob), Mrs. K's delicious homemade spinach pie with a flaky phyllo crust and the most familiar of Greek fare, gyros.

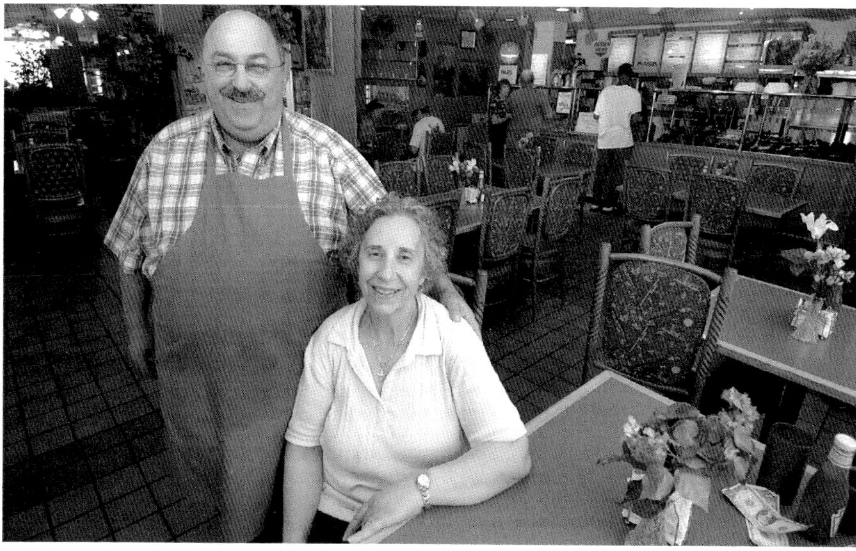

Papa John Kazas in his red apron poses with his wife, Despina, prior to Papa John's closing in May 2006. *Courtesy of the* Lincoln Journal Star.

Let's not forget Mrs. K's baklava. Her recipe is still used for the baklava served today at the Parthenon.

"I took the place and I did a very good business," Papa said. "We did all the pastries there. I did a salad bar. People loved that. People would have soup and salad."

They also loved Papa's Greek omelets. Papa tells a funny story about how he dressed up one of those Greek omelets for a regular customer.

"First time he ordered the omelet, I put some capers inside," Papa said, his eyes twinkling from the memory. "He liked them, but he didn't know what it was. The next time he came in, he said he wanted one of Papa's omelets with the Greek 'substance' inside."

That brought Papa from out of the kitchen. He couldn't have people thinking he was putting "illegal substances" in this his food.

"I told him he needed to say 'Greek spices,' and not say 'Greek substance,'" Papa said, chuckling. "I didn't need the [Lincoln Police Department] coming in and asking questions."

In 1961, Papa came to the United States as a teenager from Chios, the fifth-largest of the Greek islands in the Aegean Sea. He landed in Dubuque, Iowa, where he had relatives. That's where he met Despina, who was born in Ethiopia but raised on Chios too. They married in 1966.

Papa was working at a restaurant near a packinghouse when a group of Greek men stopped in for a sandwich. They had been buying meat from the packinghouse for their restaurant chain, Best Steak House, Papa John said. One of the men approached Papa John.

"He asked me 'Are you Italian?'" Papa said. "I said 'No.' He said 'What are you?' I said 'Close to Italian, but not Italian.'"

He liked Papa John's sense of humor and work ethic and gave him his card, telling Papa to come to Des Moines, Iowa, to check out their new store. So Papa John and his brother-in-law visited Des Moines on their day off and were impressed with what they discovered.

"We went in, and it was packed," he said. "At our place, we had soups and daily specials and we were doing this and doing that. With a steakhouse, it was a very simple thing. You make salad, baked potatoes and steaks. That's all you do. We thought it was a good idea to get out of the kitchen making all those things and to stop getting up at three or four in the morning to make breakfast. We decided to pursue this thing and go further."

Papa ended up in Ohio running a Best Steak House in Mentor, a suburb of Cleveland. He worked there until the late 1970s, when he was persuaded to leave Ohio for Iowa and take over a Bonanza. He came to Lincoln because he and Despina had relatives here.

Papa ran Papa John's with Despina and their four daughters and two sons, adding red meat to the menu after five years. As the kids grew older, they went their separate ways, leaving just Papa and Mrs. K to handle the downtown restaurant. They "retired" in May 2006, selling the restaurant.

Today, Papa and Despina sell pastries at farmers' markets or make appearances at their sons' restaurant. Their recipes continue to live on as dishes on the menu at the Parthenon.

Tastee Inn & Out

Time stood still at Tastee Inn and Out, and sometimes the traffic did too. At least it did twice: once when Lincoln's historic drive-thru celebrated its fiftieth anniversary in 1999 with fifty-cent Tastee sandwiches and then again prior to its January 2014 closing.

The former was a four-hour Sunday promotion, which coincided with a car show in the restaurant's parking lot. A line of cars stretched up 48th Street to the stoplight at Holdrege, with the Lincoln Police Department soon arriving to handle the overflow.

"I thought we were cheap to begin with, but…my Lord, they came out in hordes," Tastee's manager Linda Taylor told me for a *Lincoln Journal Star* story I wrote about the anniversary. Her father, Ben Murphy, purchased the restaurant in 1972.

Tastee, 1530 North 48th Street, actually celebrated its fifty-first birthday in 1999. It didn't mark its actual anniversary because "we didn't get around to it," Taylor said, with a chuckle.

The lines returned in late December 2013 when Taylor and her family announced Tastee was closing after sixty-five and a half years. Lincoln diners wanted to savor one last Tastee, the restaurant's signature loose-meat sandwich, and some of those famous hand-battered onion chips and dip.

Diane Walkowiak and Bill Wehrbin ordered at the counter eight days before closing and took a photo in front of the blue-and-white menu board.

"It's one of those comfortable places that didn't change much," Walkowiak told the *Journal Star*.

That was part of Tastee's charm.

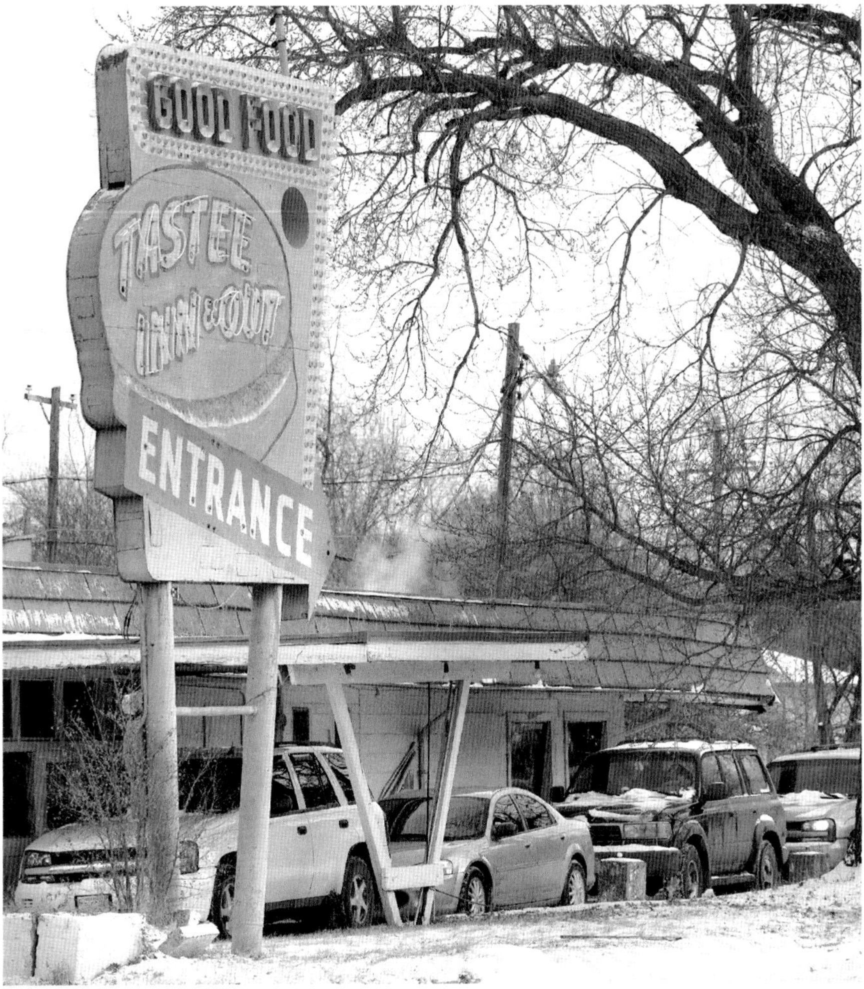

Tastee Inn & Out's drive-up window was on the passenger side of a car, one of the many things that made the drive-in unique. *Courtesy of the* Lincoln Journal Star.

Harold L. "Jug" Jorgensen sold the first Tastee sandwich for five cents at a firemen's ball in Correctionville, Iowa, in 1931. The Tastee sandwich—often replicated but never duplicated—featured ground beef, mustard and dill pickles on a bun. It was a recipe of Jorgensen's mother's, and it grew into the first Tastee Inn at 1530 North 48th Street in June 1948. After buying out his partner, Norman Tegler, Jorgensen changed the name to Tastee Inn and Out. More Tastee Inns opened in Sioux City, Iowa, and near Minneapolis.

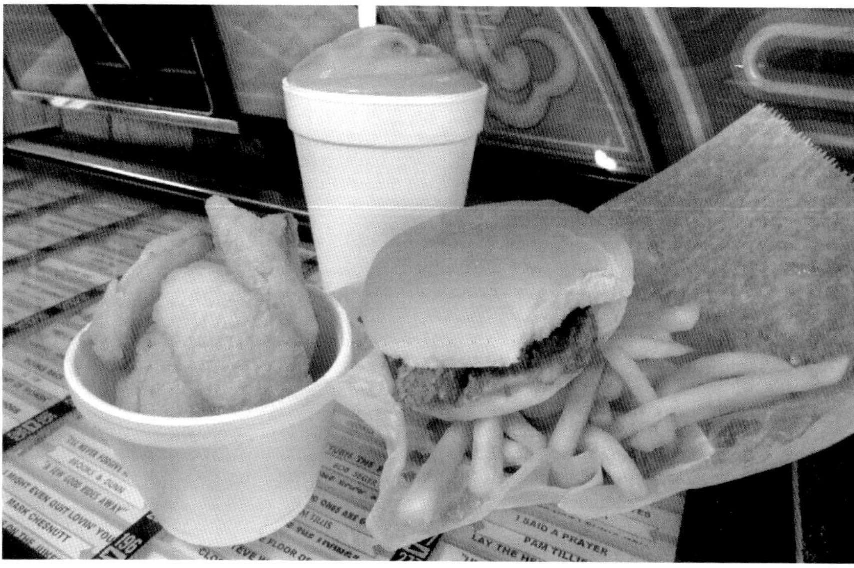

Tastee Inn & Out was known for its loose-meat sandwiches and onion chips. *Courtesy of the* Lincoln Journal Star.

In 1972, Taylor's father, Ben Murphy, bought the store. The family ran a Tastee outlet in Lincol Square at 13th and O Streets for five years but shut it down in 1992 because of low traffic and high rent.

Murphy added an atrium and restroom to the drive-in in March 1987 but changed little else. The restaurant, which seated about fifty, was known for its backward drive-thru—the pick-up window was on the passenger side of the car—and pneumatic tube, which carried orders from the front counter to the kitchen.

And then there was the sign: large, majestic and extremely retro, featuring a giant Tastee sandwich and the words "GOOD FOOD" and "ENTRANCE." At night, with its many light bulbs aglow, the sign beckoned to drivers on North 48th Street.

Tastee occasionally tinkered with its menu, adding cheese frenchee and a steak sandwich. But the heart of its lineup—the Tastee, onion chips and dip and the Tastee Pup, a hot dog smothered in a tomato-based meat sauce—never changed.

Taylor told the *Lincoln Journal* in 1995 that "within the last six years, we have switched to all-vegetable shortening, where before, we did have animal-vegetable. But with that exception, we're doing the same as we did 30 years ago, and that's it."

In 1999, the Tastee sold for $0.89, and onion chips were $1.49. When it closed in January 2014, the sandwich cost a reasonable $1.79, and onion chips were $2.85. You could get a six-pack, which is how many ordered the sandwiches, for $8.95.

Yet despite its inexpensive meals, sales declined, leading the the family to a difficult decision. Plus, the old building needed repairs, and equipment needed updating.

"I'm so sorry it had to to happen," Taylor told the *Journal Star*. "Hope you have a lot of fond memories of us."

Many do, with Tastee leaving a legacy and finding a place alongside the Yum-Yum Hut, the Mug, King's Food Host and Ken-Eddy's as classic Lincoln drive-ins.

"You know, a Tastee's a Tastee," Taylor said in 1995. "That's all there is to it."

Yum Yum Hut

No recipe has been as closely guarded or as carefully protected as that of the Yum Yum. The loose-meat sandwich was a staple of Lincoln diners for more than thirty years.

That's not to say people haven't tried to replicate it.

In 1988, as part of its "Recipe Box" feature, the *Lincoln Star* ran three recipes from readers who claimed to have perfected it. Ingredients added to the ground beef included a combination of mustard, ketchup, chili powder, horseradish, Worcestershire sauce, tomato soup, chopped onion and/or vinegar.

One reader was convinced brains and sweetbreads were added to crumbled hamburger, but "those ingredients were never advertised."

Hmmmm.

Larry Fowler, who co-owned the popular café, told the *Star* that he's had many requests over the year for the recipe, but it was copyrighted. He also said none of the recipes he had seen over those same years, all purporting to be Yum Yums, had ever been right.

Again, hmmmm.

There's no newspaper record of when Oscar Holman and Fred Kundert opened the Yum Yum Hut at 115 North 29th Street, but the men advertised the café's "formal opening" in the *Lincoln Evening Journal* and *Lincoln Star* on April 8, 1932.

The ad said the café was "introducing something new and different in tasty sandwiches" and "the ingredients in our PATENTED FORMULA combine to make a most delicious HEALTH SANDWICH."

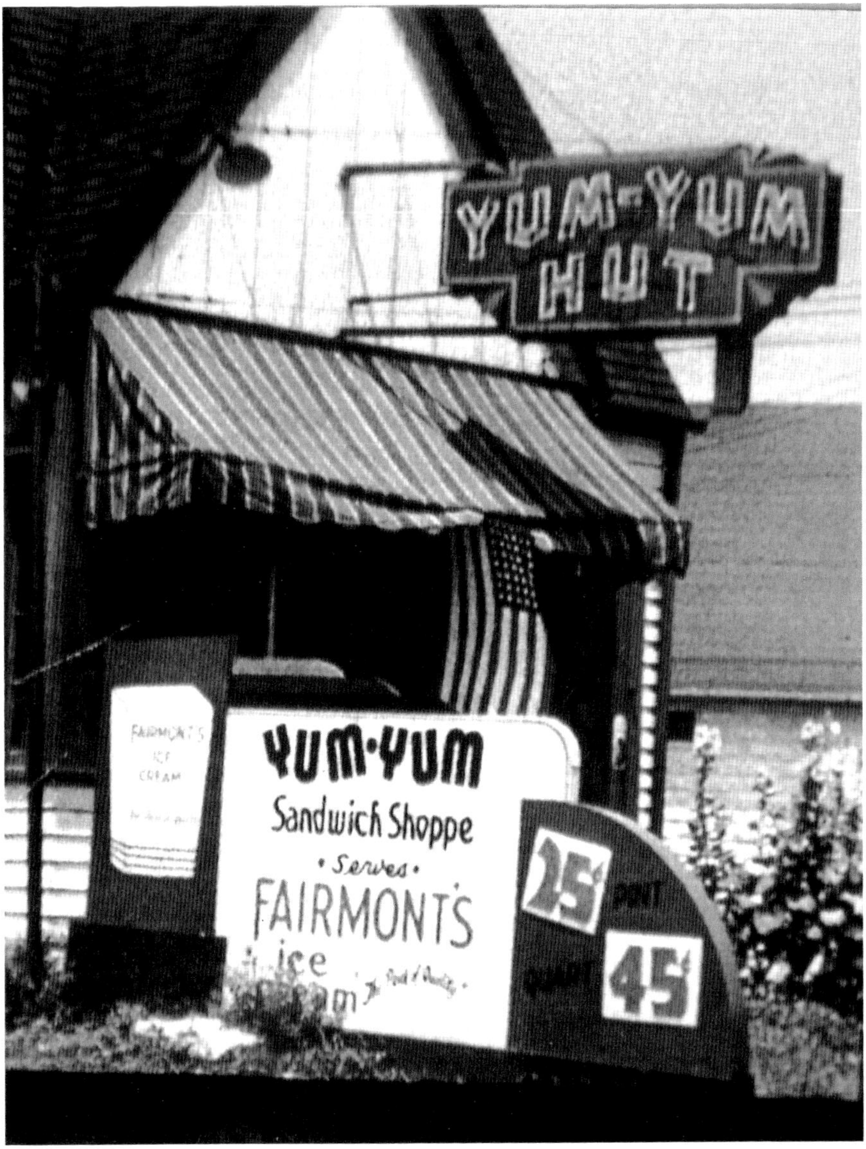

The Yum-Yum Hut at 29th and O Streets, seen here circa 1940, became so popular that police would have to direct traffic on Saturday nights to prevent O Street from jamming up. *Courtesy of Jim McKee.*

While there was no mention of sweetbreads or brains, the ad did give shout-outs to Fremont Creamery Company (for the five-cent double-dip ice cream cones), Standard Market (for the corn-fed ground beef) and Smith's Capitol Bread (for the buns).

The Yum Yum Hut would later be operated by three sisters, Kathryn Reeve, Genevieve Kundert (Fred's widow) and Margaret Holman (Oscar's widow), and their families. The Yum Yum Hut, according to Lincoln historian Jim McKee, became successful beyond anyone's dream. McKee noted in one of his newspaper columns that police had to direct traffic on Saturday nights to prevent O Street from becoming snarled.

The Yum Yum Hut closed in the mid-'60s, most likely 1966, giving way to Mr. J's Bucket barbecue joint, owned by former Nebraska football players Dennis Claridge and Rudy Johnson and basketball player Al Maxey.

But the memory of those loose-meat sandwiches lives on, although nobody—other than original owners' families—knows what was actually in them.

Bibliography

Acme Chili Parlor

Lincoln Journal. "Secret Chili Recipe Goes to New Owner." February 5, 1963.
Sunday Journal Star. "Christopulos' Special Dish: Mexican Chili." March 23, 1980.

Alice's Restaurant

Lincoln Journal. "Alice's Restaurant in College View Closing to Public." September 17, 1981.
———. "Alice's Restaurant to Be Sold, but Remain in Business." July 16, 1987.
Sunday Journal Star. "It's a New Generation for Alice's." May 26, 1974.

Bishop Buffet

Lincoln Journal. "A Line of Good Food…at Bishop Buffet." February 18, 1994.
Lincoln Journal Star. "Bishop Buffet Closes after 40 Years in Business." November 5, 1996.
Lincoln Star. "Bishop Cafeteria Joins Crowd of All-You-Can-Eat Dining Places." September 1, 1988.

Crane River

Lincoln Journal. "Crane River Offers Taste of England with Home Brew." October 23, 1992.

———. "Massive Quilt Carries Crane River's Theme." December 11, 1992.

Lincoln Star. "A Guide to Lincoln, Omaha Brewpubs." March 16, 1995.

———. "Unique Foods, Ales on Tap at Crane River Brewpub and Café." October 29, 1992.

Drumstick

Lincoln Journal. "After-Dark Personality." November 6, 1980.

———. "Legal Age, Band Fees Rise; Drumstick to Close." July 16, 1987.

Lincoln Star. "Peaceful Cafe Turns Nightclub after Dark." October 25, 1984.

Sunday Journal Star. "Venue Changes as R.E.M. Makes Its Fifth Stop in Lincoln on Oct. 3." September 24, 1989.

The Esquire Club

Lincoln Journal. "Bankruptcy Is Filed: Esquire Club Petition Told." April 9, 1971.

———. "Esquire Club Open Again." May 1, 1975.

———. "The Esquire Club Review." May 10, 1979.

Lincoln Star. "Esquire Club Makes a Triumphant Return." May 13, 1993.

Sunday Journal Star. "Esquire May Open March 21." March 5, 1972.

Grandmother's

Lincoln Journal. "Grandmother's Skillet." December 2, 1976.

Lincoln Journal Star. "Longtime Lincoln Restaurant Is Closed." February 2, 2016.

Lincoln Star. "Grandmother's Is Renamed Kerrey's." March 23, 1988.

Greenwich Cafe

Lincoln Journal. "Greenwich Eatery Closed Now, but Millie Weiler Keeps Going." October 20, 1985.

Lincoln Star. "Fish Certainly Tasty at Greenwich." June 9, 1983.

Sunday Journal Star. "Professor or Chef? Doc's Both." February 29, 1976.

Jax Shack

Lincoln Journal Star. "The Place for Special Occasions." March 9, 2001.

———. "24-Year Restaurant Jax Closes Its Doors." July 31, 2001.

Lincoln Star. "Jax Shack Name Hides Fact It's Downright Elegant." June 23, 1983.

K's Restaurant

Lincoln Journal. "Calorie Counters Need Not Play Numbers Game at K's, Alice's." October 9, 1980.

———. "K's Restaurant Might, Uh, Be in the Movies." March 2, 1983.

———. "Lions Guard Charm." May 20, 1994.

Lincoln Journal Star. "It All Came Out Oh-Kay." November 14, 1995.

Ken-Eddy's Drive-In/Eddy's Restaurant

Lincoln Journal. "A Lincoln Landmark." January 17, 1980.

Lincoln Star. "Controversial Stone Settee to Stay at 48th, O." October 3, 1950.

———. "Granting of License to Eddie Gold Upheld." February 15, 1966.

Sunday Journal Star. "Eddy's Owner Sells Restaurant at 48th, O." April 25, 1984.

———. "Eddy's Restaurant Gone but Not Forgotten." March 11, 1988.

King's Food Host

Lincoln Journal. "Single Group to Own Jim King Enterprises, Food Host U.S.A." June 8, 1972.

Lincoln Journal Star. "Lincoln Developer Price Remembered for Generosity." August 28, 1999.
Lincoln Star. "Hot Grill, Dream Pay Off for Larry Price." November 22, 1964.
———. "Lincoln Restaurateur Put Initiative to Work in Successful Career." February 21, 1983.
McKee, Jim. "Tuna Frenchee, King's Lives One." *Lincoln Journal Star*, December 6, 2009.

The Knolls Restaurant

Lincoln Evening Journal. "Capital City Will Get First Par 3 Golf Course." October 17, 1961.
Lincoln Journal Star. "Auction Offers Piece of the Knolls." October 28, 2015.
———. "The Knolls a Country Club Restaurant Open to the Public." June 15, 2001.
Lincoln Star. "Knolls Still Fighting Assumption It's for Country Club Members Only." September 6, 1984.

Kuhl's Restaurant

Lincoln Journal. "Kuhl's Is a Lincoln Institution." March 3, 1983.
Lincoln Journal Star. "Kuhl's Restaurant Closing after Lease Not Renewed." October 28, 2007.
———. "Regulars Reflect on Restaurant's Family Atmosphere as It Serves Its Final Meals." March 17, 2008.

Lebsack Brothers Tavern

Lincoln Journal. "Lebsack's Chili at Barrymore's Rated Good Copy by Two-Alarmer." January 17, 1985.
Raglin, Jim. *Lincoln Journal*, August 1978.
Sunday Journal Star. "Lebsack's—Where You Can Imbibe in Fun and Ingest." August 25, 1974.

Legionnaire Club

Lincoln Evening Journal. "Legionnaire Club Buying Italian Village Building." January 26, 1960.

Lincoln Journal Star. "Last Call for the Legionnaire Club." August 29, 2002.

Lincoln Exchange

Exchange. "Food and Thought." October 1980.

Lincoln Journal. "Lincoln Exchange Closed Oct. 18." October 29, 1986.

Lincoln Star. "Exchange Hopes to Become Meeting Spot." October 16, 1980.

———. "Regulars Relieved Lincoln Exchange Is Back in Business." October 10, 1985.

Lincoln Underground/Brittany's

Lincoln Journal. "Play Time." October 14, 1976

Lincoln Star. "Northern Italian Restaurant to Replace Lincoln Underground in Haymarket." August 8, 1991.

———. "$750,00 Project Revealed." May 12, 1983.

———. "Underground Brings Back Menu, Memories." May 14, 1991

———. "Victorian-Style Restaurant Opens." September 8, 1983.

Miller & Paine Tea Room

Campbell, Bob. "A History of Miller & Paine, Its Founder and Entrepreneur, J.E. Miller, His Family and Their Enterprises." Presentation for a Lincoln woman's group.

Lincoln Journal Star. "Downtown Tearoom Serves Last Public Meal." February 9, 1991.

———. "Legends of the Roll: Arne Pederson Still Making Magic with Miller & Paine Cinnamon Rolls." June 10, 2007.

McKee, Jim. "Lunch at Miller & Paine Tea Room." *Lincoln Journal Star*, November 9, 1997.

The Mug

Sunday Journal Star. "The Mug: Root Beer Stand at 33rd and O Looked Like a Human Face." August 6, 1978.

———. "Nebelsick, Fast-Food Pioneer, Dies." July 30, 1982.

Norma's Place

Lincoln Journal Star. "Norma's in Danger of Closing." April 5, 2002.

Papa John's

Lincoln Journal Star. "Papa Is Hanging Up the Red Apron." May 26, 2006.

———. "Papa John's Greek Eatery Has Endured for Good Reason." December 29, 2000.

P.O. Pears

Lincoln Journal Star. "Kiss 'Em Goodbye." April 19, 2008.

———. "25 and Counting: With Burgers, Music and Giant Lips, P.O. Pears Is Going Strong after a Quarter Century." September 2, 2005.

Reuben's

Lincoln Journal. "Coco's Offering Limited Dinner Fare from Former Reuben's." February 27, 1986.

Lincoln Star. "Reuben's Prime Rib Is Excellent." April 14, 1983.

Los Angeles Times. "W.R. Grace Agrees to Buy Far West Services." September 9, 1970.

Sunday Journal Star. "Reuben's Opens at Gateway." January 9, 1972.

The Rotisserie

Lincoln Journal. "In the Grotto." July 8, 1994.

———. "Rotisserie Is 'Luxe' Restaurant." December 17, 1981.
Lincoln Journal Star. "Remembering a Waiter Extraordinaire." February 4, 2011.
———. "Restaurant and Bar Owner Nader Sepahpur Always Changing." February 26, 2017.
———. "Service with a Smile…and Then Some." July 21, 2000.
Lincoln Star. "Rotisserie Restaurant Has Touch of Elegance." December 18, 1981.

Skylight Bistro

Lincoln Journal. "Bistro Restaurant Has Closed." September 30, 1991.
———. "Skylight Bistro Is Superb-O." April 8, 1982.
———. "Skylight Bistro Renewed." September 8, 1983.
Lincoln Star. "Attention to Detail Makes Bistro Special." January 11, 1990.
———. "Bigger, Better Bistro Expected to Open Downtown on Sunday." December 28, 1989.
———. "Bistro Aims to Match Service to Food Quality." May 26, 1988.

The Steak House

Lincoln Journal Star. "A Lot at Steak: Lincoln Fixture the Steak House Celebrates 50 Years." July 2, 1999
———. "The Steak House Is Closed, after 65 Years." December 23, 2014.

Taco Hut/Arturo's

Lincoln Journal Star. "Adios, Arturo's." June 9, 2007.
———. "Arturo's Closes with Strange, Abrupt End." June 15, 2007.
———. "Arturo's Makes Triumphant Comeback Downtown." October 30, 1998.

Tastee Inn & Out

Lincoln Journal. "A Tastee's a Tastee—Since Mid-1948." May 19, 1995.

Lincoln Journal Star. "Lincoln Landmark Tastee Inn to Close." December 28, 2013.
———. "Tastee Celebrates 50 Years Serving Lincoln." June 4, 1999.
Lincoln Star. "Founder of Tastee Drive Inn Dies." July 28, 1981.

Tony and Luigi's

Lincoln Evening Journal. "Tony's, Lee's Open for Business 30 Years." September 26, 1975.
Lincoln Journal. "Longtime Italian Restaurant Closing." May 21, 1993.
———. "Tony Alesio Ending 33 Years of Operating Tony and Luigi's." June 28, 1978.
Lincoln Star. "Dual Restaurant, Club Operation 'Not Illegal.'" October 25, 1963.
———. "A Facelift…and Even More for an Old Lincoln Favorite." October 1, 1987.
———. "A Lincoln Tradition to End as Tony and Luigi's Closes." May 21, 1993.

Interviews

Alesio, Mike, and Tony Messineo. Tony and Luigi's, October 24, 2017.
Brestel, Kay. K's Restaurant, December 15, 2017.
Campbell, Bob. Miller & Paine Tea Room, November 6, 2017.
Jergensen, Bob. P.O. Pears, January 29, 2018.
Kann, Diane, and Mark Lohmeier. Drumstick, December 4, 2017.
Kazas, John, and Despina Kazas. Papa John's, October 23, 2017.
Kuhl, Pearl. Kuhl's Restaurant, October 13, 2017.
Logsdon, Rob. Legionnaire Club, December 19, 2017.
Longoria, Rene, and Daniel Longoria. Taco Hunt/Arturo's, January 4, 2018.
Pleskac, Maggie. Maggie's Vegetarian Café, January 19, 2018.
Sepahpur, Nader. The Rotisserie, December 1, 2017.
Smith, Matt. Grandmother's, January 23, 2018.
Tiebel, Kristina. Crane River, December 14, 2017.

About the Author

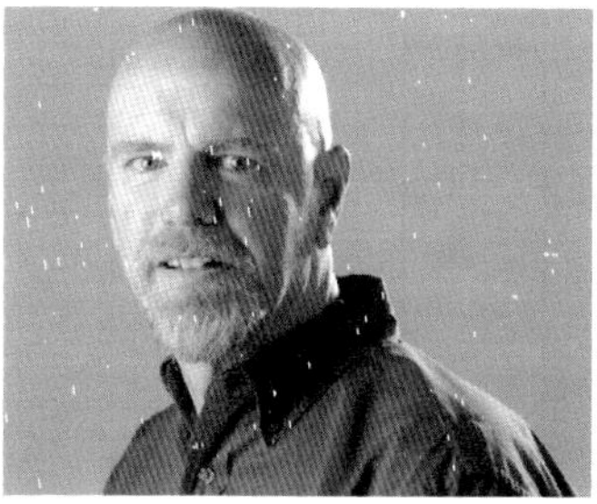

Jeff Korbelik ate at and wrote about restaurants for more than twenty years at the *Lincoln Journal Star*. He originally wanted to be a starting pitcher for the New York Mets or a running back for the New York Jets, but with no athletic ability, outside of a deep passion for sports, he turned to writing about them. He spent ten years as a sports journalist, covering three Nebraska football national championships for the *Grand Island Independent* and *Lincoln Journal Star* before switching gears and joining the features staff at the *Journal Star* as an entertainment reporter. Since 1998, he covered dining, performing arts, television and radio for the newspaper. He served as features editor from 2012 to 2017 before leaving the newspaper to pursue another business opportunity. He lives in Lincoln with his wife and frequent dining companion, Rebecca; makes a mean omelet, pot of chili and pan of lasagna; and continues to follow the Mets, Jets and the Huskers (of course). This is his first book.